Anne Va

ART *and* SOUL

Exploring God's Power Through Scripture and Creative Arts

Abingdon Press / Nashville

Art and Soul:
Exploring God's Power Through Scripture and Creative Arts

by Anne Van Dillen Roth

Copyright © 2002 by Abingdon Press

This book is printed on acid-free paper.

ISBN 0-687-04512-6

02 03 04 05 06 07 08 09 10 11—10 9 8 7 6 5 4 3 2 1

MANUFACTURED IN THE UNITED STATES OF AMERICA

Contents

About the Author 4

A Word of Welcome 5

Chapter One: The Power of Creation
   Genesis 1:1–2:3 8

Chapter Two: The Power of Healing
   2 Kings 5:1-19 20

Chapter Three: The Power of Trust
   Mark 4:35-41 34

Chapter Four: The Power of Resurrection
   John 20:1-18 47

Chapter Five: The Power of Spiritual Community
   Acts 2:1-43 60

About the Author

$\mathcal{A}$nne Van Dillen Roth spent ten years as a United Methodist pastor in the Southern New Jersey Annual Conference before moving with her husband, Bill, to California. For the next several years, she worked with an agency caring for persons living with HIV. That work included five years of writing interviews of the clients, staff, and volunteers for their newsletter. Over the past five years, Anne has spent increasing amounts of time helping with the creation of the United Religions Initiative. She has served as Conference staff for four of the global summits. With the 2001 emphasis on regional development, Anne has been made Chair of the Committee for Cooperation Circle Development and Nurture for URI North America. Her interfaith work extends from local connections to the Board of the county Interfaith Council, which has also become a Cooperation Circle of URI.

Anne's undergraduate work focused on history and music. She graduated from New Brunswick Theological Seminary with honors. She has continued her education with a Certificate in Spiritual Direction. Anne is a freelance teacher for local congregations of various traditions and has offered such workshops as "Bridging the Gap Between Religion and Spirituality" and "Walking a Christian Path in the Global Community." She has previously published studies with Cokesbury in two series: CHALLENGE and SCRIPTURES FOR THE CHURCH SEASONS.

A Word of Welcome

Welcome to ART AND SOUL: EXPLORING GOD'S POWER THROUGH SCRIPTURE AND CREATIVE ARTS. This five-session study will introduce you to several biblical instances of God's awesome power. It can be used in conjunction with *God's Great Gallery: Exploring God's Wonderful Works* material for children and youth, but it is also a significant stand-alone study that we think you will find inspiring and helpful.

Power is a tricky subject in our day. We have been made aware of the damage that can be done by people who are hungry for power, people too much addicted to power and control over others. We have emerged from a century in which power games and power mongering among the nations have played an enormous part in Earth's history. That kind of power is external; it is the kind of power that inherently powerless people have.

The contrast is visible in those whose power is internal—interior, faith based, ethical. People in touch with their self-esteem rather than their egos are grounded and centered, people who have accepted themselves as God made them and committed themselves to use their gifts for the highest good. For such people, we use words like integrity and faithfulness. Such people get offered power; they rarely seek it.

Above and beyond all the kinds of human power lies the power of God, the power that is God. God's power is described for us in the Bible by stories in which God has chosen to break into the lives of real people who are not "perfect" or "acceptable" by human social standards. We call those mighty acts of God "miracles" because we cannot understand how or why such a powerful God might choose to reach out and touch creation to shift or to save.

5

When we look at the stories in Scripture that show us the creativity of God, we realize that they may have become so familiar to us that they have lost the impact of an initial encounter. These sessions offer the possibility of looking again at well-known stories with new wonder, seeing God's hand in people's lives with the awe of our inner, faithful child who yearns for the "WOW!" response.

When we read the first Creation story in Genesis 1:1–2:3, it is a laundry list of the order in which God chose to layer a void with forms of life. What was God's reason for shaping land and waters? Where do we find the awe in the way this process is described? How do we understand the God-given gift of creativity in us?

In the historical records of Second Kings, we are told the story of a general who suffered from leprosy, the most dreaded disease of his time. On the suggestion of a slave girl, he undertook a journey carrying a great deal of wealth to pay for a healing. Where is the wonder of God's power in this story? What is it that heals? What is healing?

The story in the Gospel of Mark narrates the amazement of Jesus' companions as he calmed the storm that nearly destroyed their boat at sea. Where is the deeper awe beneath and behind this tale? Why might it have been included in the canon?

Early in the morning, when Mary found an empty tomb, she wept with grief. The stranger she assumed was the gardener revealed his identity to her with one word: her name. There is more than a miracle of resurrection in this story. There is a depth of reconnection that evokes awe. How can we understand again the lives we have lived in terms of this story?

In the earliest days of floundering for guidance after the loss of their teacher, the disciples gathered in the upper room. Flames awakened them to move into a future they could never have imagined. Peter shared the wonder of his sudden understanding. How do the pieces fall together in our understanding? How do past Scripture and future life mesh? Where is the wind of their empowerment blowing in our lives?

Can we free our imagination to see old stories in new ways and renew our relationship with the power that is God?

A Few Tips on This Resource

ART AND SOUL has several design features to help you have a satisfying learning experience and prepare a suitable teaching plan. The main text includes commentary on the biblical text with further thoughts on its meaning and application for us. In the narrow margin on the left side of the page, you will find teaching helps, beginning in each chapter with a purpose statement for the session and a reminder of how the teaching options are identified.

ART AND SOUL is suitable for an intergenerational teaching setting, such as vacation Bible school, which may meet for 2 hours or more, or for a "typical" 45-60 minute study session on Sunday morning or some other study setting. To help you decide how to select the activities that will work best in your setting, note the way the activities are identified.

Understanding the Design

Activities identified with ❖ indicate those teaching suggestions that form the core or main learning for a session. Every section in the main text has at least one core option, which is on the left side of the page, with the same, or an abbreviated, subhead as the section to which it refers. Choose from among these core activities, which can be done in just about any meeting space with only a Bible and the study book.

Activities in bold italics need extra time or preparation to do and may also require added resources, such as a Bible atlas, dictionary, or commentary. These can be used if you have time and can obtain the needed study tools or art supplies.

Enjoy!

ART AND SOUL is designed to encourage you to use your creativity to experience and appreciate the wonder of God. We hope you free your sense of play and awe and take a sense of delight in the arts as they help reveal both the God of power and the God within.

7

Chapter One

The Power of Creation
Genesis 1:1–2:3

PURPOSE
This session is an invitation to see with new eyes the complex and interdependent ways that God set free patterns of creativity in a world of wonder.

THE SESSION PLAN
Choose from among the core teaching activities (identified with ❖) and add options in **bold italics** to extend beyond a 45-60 minute session.

FIRESIDE TALES
❖ Read Genesis 1:1–2:3 and stop at each "day" to reflect upon or discuss how these elements have enriched your understanding of God's power in the world.

Fireside Tales

"In the beginning. . . ." *Beresit bara.*

Over the centuries since these words were put together and this story told, then written, people have often wondered, *Which beginning? When? Where? How?* English-speaking Christians have defended—sometimes passionately—whatever their concept of "the beginning" was about. Yet in the original Hebrew, there is no definite article. The Hebrew says, "in a beginning" or "some beginning" or, as we might say to the children, "Once upon a time."

The New Interpreter's Bible (Abingdon, 1994, Volume I, page 337) refers to such thinking as "pre-scientific" but affirms both the matter of faith and the first attempts at ordering and classification. Not until the seventeenth century did the world produce a full-blown scientific classification of plants by genus, species, and variety.

Creation stories can be understood in a way as "fireside tales." Do you remember the first time you sat with your par-

❖ After the Scripture reading, consider these questions: When have you watched a major rainstorm and thought about the separation of waters? When have you celebrated the bounty of a garden? When have the flights of birds awakened your wonder? Which aspect of Creation draws your interest most? Are you a person who needs to spend time in nature in order to feel centered?

Have a campfire with the children and let them tell you their theological understandings of the world and its creation. Ask them to share their own experiences of nature. How do they see God in the world?

❖ If a campfire is not possible, have an intergenerational gathering and create small circles of people of various ages. Make a fire ring with an artificial log so all can gather around it. Share with one another experi-

ent—or with your child—at a campfire or fireplace and let the dancing flames awaken curiosity? Perhaps that child wanted to know, "What's out there where it's dark? How does fire work? Why is the sky blue? What did that lady mean when she said I was found in a cabbage patch? How did God make me?"

Over the millennia, humans have gathered around kindling light and warmth to share their stories. In her book *Seeing in the Dark* (Abingdon, 2001, page 18), Bishop Beverly Shamana teaches us the Ashante word *Sankofa,* which is a conceptual bridge between past and future, the honoring of past wisdom in building the future. Honoring the past does not mean barricading ourselves there; it is a source of fuel and food for moving forward into new creation.

Children's questions run deep when their imagination is not yet fettered by "Don't say that." I took a six-year-old to dinner one night; and she opened the conversation by asking, "Who was here first?" Confused, I asked, "You mean who was in the restaurant before us?" "No. Who was here first?" "Who lived in this town before we arrived?" "NO! Who was here first?" (very annoyed by now at my dim wits) It dawned on me. "Who were the first people on earth?" "Yes."

So I told her the Creation story about how God made people. Her response: "That's dumb." So I explained a little bit about evolution. That sounded dumb to her, too. I replied that those were her current choices, and she would have to do

ences you have had in nature. How has the Bible enriched your understanding of the world?

her own research if she wanted a better answer. That conversation happened twenty-five years ago. Now and then I think about that child and wonder what answers she found that suited her. For in truth we are caught somewhere between these two versions.

Faith or Science?

Carl Sagan gave us a more up-to-date look at the concepts and pathways of evolution in *Shadows of Forgotten Ancestors* (Ballantine, 1993). A generation before him, a Roman Catholic priest and paleontologist, Pierre Teilhard de Chardin, gave us the powerful theory that evolution itself is driven and empowered by Spirit (See *The Phenomenon of Man,* Perennial, 1975.). Faith? Or Science? Or both?

Pre-scientific or not, there is order in the process of the Genesis account of Creation. First, light. Nothing can grow without sunshine, and nothing can thrive continually without rest. My husband reminded me, "You need a light on your workbench." "And there was evening and . . . morning, the first day" (Genesis 1:5).

There was a separation of waters, a three-story world explained by people who had never flown above a cloud. If you have ever stood in a downpour of heavy rain, you know how hard it is to breathe. So, above the sky, the sweet waters were gathered (They fall down, don't they?); and the salt waters stayed underneath. Some Native American tra-

FAITH OR SCIENCE?
❖ Stage a debate between proponents of each viewpoint. Be sure to allow both sides time to be heard so that the class can understand the creative tension between them. Where has the tension revealed itself in American society between an uncritical reliance on science or a limited understanding of the Bible?

For an extended session, choose from among the following options.

Stargaze
Spend 15 minutes or so tonight, or when the weather next permits, to sit outside and gaze at the stars. Reflect on how this nighttime view offers its own perspective on God's work. Then offer a prayer of thanksgiving for the created order.

Sailors
Describe how landfall appears on a watery horizon. Can you understand why the Native Americans called the land what they did?

Take a nature walk
and notice how the plants crowd together or make room for each to reach the light.

Plant a class garden
and share the bounty with your local food bank. Have people with backyard gardens bring in their extras to share with your congregation. Take the money they exchange and the extras to the food bank.

Tell how science fiction books or movies
have enriched your understanding of the universe. In what ways has their creative approach to "new worlds" added to your ability to be creative in seeing this world?

Take a trip to the zoo.
Enjoy again the wonder of all the unique creatures God has made.

ditions refer to the earth's surface as Turtle Island. In between, air to breathe. A second day.

Slosh the seas into the low spots and let there be dry land. Sweet water plus dry land plus seed plus sunshine equal food—all kinds of vegetation. Goodness. Edible goodness. A third day.

In the process of a child's growing, there are stages of awareness, too. What is next? Look up. There is a show better than any music video, one that cannot be canceled by any network management. During the past half century of scientific research and even science fiction, we have been given a whole new understanding of the potential universe. What an amazing sky! A place of dreams and adventure and more suns and worlds than we can ever explore, no matter how far we "boldly go." A fourth day.

With the dry land covered in goodness, God turned to the sea and filled it with living creatures from plankton to "great sea monsters" (Genesis 1:21). And the sky was filled with birds of all kinds. A fifth day. Goodness and blessing. Even the pharmaceutical companies are turning to the sea to find compounds and substances that cure all kinds of illnesses.

On the sixth day, the creatures of the land came forth—wild life. "And it was so" (Genesis 1:24). When was the last time you visited a zoo and noticed the wonderful shapes and colors, the infinite variety, the amazing artwork of God? But God was not finished yet. What might this world look like today if God had decided this was enough? What if God had stopped here in the story?

THE HUMAN DYNAMIC
❖ If you were God, how would you design a creature (including a human being)? What would it need to survive in its environment? Draw a picture of one and discuss the reasoning behind your choices. See if you can grasp why the Native Americans found such spiritual learning in the creatures around them. What have you learned from your relationship with a pet?

The Human Dynamic

While I was in seminary, a friend who was studying hymns ran across an idea that intrigued her. She asked me, "If God made angels first and angels are perfect, why did God bother to make humans?" My fanciful mind responded with this: "Angels are God's messengers. If you send an angel out for coffee, you know you'll always get it back hot with the right amount of cream and sugar. If you send a human out for coffee, you never know what you'll get. Maybe God created humans so God wouldn't be bored." In all the years since then, it has been my delight or occasional anguish to notice all the ways in which humans keep God from getting bored.

"So God created humankind" (Genesis 1:27), and few have been bored since. Having made all these intricate living things and endowed them with the power to reproduce, to multiply, why would God give the last-formed creatures dominion over it all? With foresight God must have realized the potential danger of undisciplined multiplication. Creativity without discipline is like uncontrolled nuclear fission or cell division without order.

By recognizing greatness in the disciplined arts, we intuitively acknowledge that implicit truth. Such recognition may also fuel our fascination with the fractal

Have someone with a computer and a fractal generator show the class how the iterations develop. If you click and drag on sections of the pattern and blow them up, you can see that the unique aspects of each equation are repeated in infinite variety and detail level after level.

❖ In small groups, spend a few minutes describing what you feel are the best qualities of the opposite sex. Then describe what you consider to be the best qualities of your own gender. What do these descriptions reveal about your beliefs of "traditional," gender-based attributes and roles?

Read Genesis 1:26-31 and 2:7-9, 15-25. How would you describe the purpose and roles of the man and woman with God, creation, and each other?

Any there any fathers in the class who are the primary caregivers in the family? Are there any professional women? Describe your journey and feelings about your role. How has your understanding of the classic relig-

art that comes from Chaos Theory mathematics. With the available speed of computers, it is now possible for mathematicians to follow the intricate multiplying of an equation through thousands of steps to discover the actual visual patterns of replication and iteration. These visual patterns are familiar by their appearance in all phases of nature, from leaf veins to human cells. Is this the patterning God intended? Have we discovered the clue?

"Male and female" (Genesis 1:27). The social separation of genders over the centuries worked on the surface. It is only in the past century that psychologists have begun to understand that this phrase refers to an internal wholeness of each human being. Each of us is both male and female, and we live out that balance in different ways. The Taoists call it "yang and yin"—the male and female energies of life. It is a symbol of wholeness and balance.

What happens along the pathways of life is that we actually take turns living out of the different energies. There are times in all people's lives when they live out what are described as male roles or female roles. And it is at about mid-life that those roles or "energies" switch— that a man who has been cerebral and exterior and functional begins to turn inward and value his family more and long to teach or nurture. It is at about that time that a woman who may have spent her early years raising children and being willing to limit her arena because of that gets restless and wants to tackle a

ious perceptions of gender roles changed with your living experience?

❖ What evidence do you see in your own creative endeavors of the "holy birthmark" from God? How does your understanding and appreciation of your own creative abilities (you do have them) help you receive or understand God's purpose for you in the universal scheme of things?

GOD TALK
❖ Review Rabbi Lerner's description of God. How would you restate his comments? How does the concept of God as a verb or a process square with your understanding of God's identity? What is your own personal definition of God?

new job or a more challenging situation. She wants to be taken seriously in the business world as well.

Some of us actually do it the other way around. I am a woman who had an early career and has spent the years since I turned forty being more inward and more domestic. My husband at forty moved from his inward-turning journey out into a more challenging position, a new career.

No matter how we live it out, the balance is terribly necessary to our spiritual wholeness and therefore to our physical, mental, and emotional wholeness. Beverly Shamana notes, "We are the offspring of a creative God whose hand print is stamped indelibly on our soul, marking us for continuing creativity in the world. This holy birthmark is the Creator's personal gift to the universe for all time" (*Seeing in the Dark,* page 12).

God Talk

Rabbi Michael Lerner in *Spirit Matters* (Hampton Roads, 2000, page 47) gives us this definition:

When I talk of God, I am talking about YHVH (mistranslated in the King James version as Jehovah, but actually four letters that Jews never pronounced precisely because they do not signify a specific being, but a world process, a God-ing . . . a *Verb*). YHVH comes from the root HVH, the Hebrew word for 'the present tense' and the Y, which indicates the future. What the word really

14

means is 'the transformation of the present into that which can and should be in the future.' In this sense, God is the Power of Healing and Transformation in the universe—and the Voice of the Future calling us to become who we need to become.

Recall God's words to Moses at the sight of the bush, burning but not consumed: "I AM WHO I AM," or "I WILL BE WHAT I WILL BE" (Exodus 3:14).

"And God said. . . ." The key to these passages springs from the concept hidden in the Hebrew word *dabar.* God spoke, and the thing happened. The creative potential is all one idea.

If we take seriously the gift of the creative God to include us in creation, to include us as co-creators, what does that mean to us? Yes, we are empowered to explore and make and do. We are given the gift that what we make may be deemed "good." We are also given the perception to know when something we make may be judged "bad." The spiritual balance is in discerning the difference.

We are also gifted with the power of speaking, and speaking creates realities. What we say matters. Blessings matter. Curses matter. The good will or negativity that proceeds from our mouths matters. Jesus said, "Listen and understand: it is not what goes into the mouth that defiles a person, but it is what comes out of the mouth that defiles" (Matthew 15:10-11).

In his seminal work *Appreciative Inquiry* (Stipes Publishing L.L.C., 2000, page 30), Dr. David Cooperrider of Case Western says, "To a far greater extent

❖ Consider *dabar,* the term that reflects the creative dimension of God's speaking. God speaks and something happens. Is that creative activity open to human persons as well?

❖ Form three teams, and among them read Matthew 15:10-11, Deuteronomy 28:1-45, and James 3:1-12. How does what comes from our mouths either work for or against the purposes of God? How do our words bring forth good or evil? build up or tear down? bless or curse? create life or destroy it? How does this awesome ability teach you about the power of words to form, transform, and deform?

❖ Brainstorm a class list of the blessings you want to send out into your church, your community, and your nation.

❖ Journal privately an experience of cursing or being cursed and how that influenced your spiritual understanding. What Bible story of cursing helped your understanding?

than is normally acknowledged, we human beings create our own realities through symbolic and mental processes."

A century of psychoanalysis has given us endless windows into the damage done by careless tongues. Our ego-based, automatic reactions to our children when we were distracted by some pressure have left scars we would never have intended. But we have not paid attention to that God-given gift of creating reality. All good spiritual direction begins with self-observation. What is it we are saying? And do those words come from ego or from spirit? What motivates our tongue to say some of the things we say? And once we begin to perceive, why are we surprised when our negativity comes back at us?

THE CREATIVE GIFT
❖ What has been your avenue of creativity? Share with the group your gifts in music or art, your interests, your poetry. How has your faith fed your creativity? How has your creativity fed your faith?

Sing hymns of Creation. Explore your hymnal for Creation hymns and sing or say several of them together. How do the music and lyrics inspire you? reveal God to you? help you under-

The Creative Gift

In more visible ways, our gift of co-creativity comes out in the myriad arts that have blossomed over the centuries. What has been your experience when faced with an exquisite painting or a thrilling piece of music? How have the hymns of Charles Wesley fed your spirit and given poetry to your soul? When have you looked with wonder upon a graceful bridge or an impressive building? Have you ever visited or seen a picture of the Spanish cathedral *La Sagrada Familia,* which is an architectural wonder? Which authors have deepened your spiritual life with words of wisdom?

A man in California has taken these

16

stand your own place in creation and your own creative abilities?

❖ On a piece of paper, draw a two-headed arrow. At each end, write the pieces of your own life that have been a paradox or tension for you, for instance, the struggle to keep a balance between work and family or the tug-of-war between taking care of others and maintaining your own spiritual health. On a second page, write your name in the center; then draw arrows outward from it. Label each one for the person with whom you work to maintain a relationship—your children, spouse, parents. Make an arrow for your job, your church, your schooling, and your projects. Then look at the whole collection and discern where the tug and pull is out of balance for you. What emphasis do you need in life to get you back into balance?

understandings to a new place of development. The Reverend Matthew Fox has opened his University of Creation Spirituality in Oakland. The school offers academic programs at the graduate level. "Creation Spirituality is a movement that integrates the wisdom of the world's great spiritual traditions with creativity and the new cosmology, providing a solid foundation and sacred perspective to address the complex issues of our time," says a course description in their public flyer. Another course uses the term *autopoiesis* as "to be is to be a center of creativity." How often have we seen ourselves as a "center of creativity"?

We live most fully in a place of creative tension. Draw a two-headed arrow and think about the paradoxes in your life that might fit at the opposite ends of that balance. If there is too little tension, life sags like a tightrope that is too loose to walk upon. If there is too much tension in the tightrope, the rope will bounce us right off its surface. In these United States, we live with the creative tension between faith and science.

This point of balance is being explored by physicians who have rediscovered the role of prayer in healing and by HMO's who are waking up to the statistics that show that people who belong to a praying community heal faster. This fact has been a constant in the awareness of practitioners of alternatives to standard medicine who deal with patients under both kinds of care.

There are people who have begun to explore the relationship between technol-

17

ogy and spirituality, looking for ways to re-instill ethics into a soul-less technology. Tom Mahon of www.reconnecting.com has produced several articles on the subject as well as a wonderful one-man play about creation called "Are We Having Fun Yet?"

What has been your experience with having a community of prayer support you in a time of need? How did that make a difference in your journey? Or, if you did not have anyone there when you needed such support, how was that for you?

The incredible work of God in creating a world of beauty and power, of edible goodness, of light and shadow, of wonders in the heavens and in the deeps, is echoed again in us. We have light and shadow within us. We have beauty and power. That may be why we refer to some people as "stars." We see again in our children the rhythms of energy and rest, of growing and swimming and joy.

CELEBRATING THE WHOLE
Plan an Earth Day Service for next spring. Write your own litany around the lesson from Genesis that can be used in worship as a responsive prayer. Choose hymns that speak to your understanding of your role in the stewardship of the earth.

Celebrating the Whole

In the new understanding of ideas like *Sankofa*, people around the world are gathering in circles to share their stories, to learn one another's faith journey, to discover together the human creativity that can work together for good rather than making walls that divide. The United Religions Initiative is growing with Cooperation Circles all over the world that gather together people of different faiths to seek creative solutions for the

Add a project for the whole community. One community uses a long chain-link fence in a public park for everyone to tie bookmark-sized prayer papers on the fence. Others do clean-up projects or paint a house for individuals who cannot afford to do it themselves.

Close this chapter by singing "God of the Sparrow, God of the Whale."

future. Communities of prayer are coming to recognize the shared roots of God's presence while enjoying the diversity of the humanly created surface differences. And in the process, the old wisdom is being celebrated again in balanced wholeness.

Chapter Two

The Power of Healing
2 Kings 5:1-19

PURPOSE
To learn how to see the power of God in the life journeys and healing of humankind.

THE SESSION PLAN
Choose from among the core teaching activities (identified with ❖) and add options in **bold italics** to extend beyond a 45-60 minute session.

INTO THE PICTURE
❖ Read 2 Kings 5:1-19. Choose the micro-scene that interests you the most. Why did you choose that piece? What was it that caught your attention?

Paint your own vision of what Damascus looked like. Or request pictures and a "travelogue" from someone who has been there.

Walk Into the Picture

Imagine the scene: set in the oldest continuously inhabited city on Earth, a great warren of twisted streets filled with houses that look down upon them with blank faces. Imagine swinging open the gate that leads into an inner courtyard filled with flowering shrubs and citrus trees around a central fountain. See the balconies of the second story that surround it, the household servants in their loosely flowing garments moving about doing their appointed tasks. This is the home of an important man—the general of the king's armies.

Walk behind the chariot of the king's general, the commander of the victorious army at the battle in Ramoth-gilead in northern Israel. The chariot turns onto the great Street called Straight, the heart of Damascus in Aram/Syria. The city had once been subjugated by David when he was king of a united Israel; but after Solomon's demise, the division into two smaller kingdoms shifted the balance of power in that world. Damascus was not to fall again until Assyria took it in 732 B.C.

Show slides of Syria/Israel and imagine yourself living there. How would the news today affect your choice of where to live?

❖ Look up "leprosy" in a Bible dictionary. How did such a disease determine the shape of that society? (See Leviticus 13.) How did Jesus' ministry to these "outcasts" demonstrate his talent for healing? Who are the "lepers" in our society? How do we exclude them? What kind of behaviors mark for people in a community who is "in" and who is "out"?

❖ Discuss the credibility of information that you receive from "alternative sources," such as the slave girl. How do you view such facts? What sources might parallel her role? How do you feel about giving credence to them? to acting upon their advice?

LIFE CHALLENGES
❖ Share pictures and stories of people you have loved who have battled with diseases

In its ascendancy in the ninth century, it was—as it is today—a great trading center for dried fruit, wine, leather, wool, linen, silk, and filigreed jewelry of gold and silver. Damask was the name of the earliest of patterned woven silks.

Follow the path of this proud and important man in the rich robes of a king's favorite. Look with horror upon the peeling skin of his face and arms, skin darkened by the Mediterranean sun and outdoor campaigns, peeling away to leave patches of white flesh and tatters where the itch drove him to scratch. Leprosy? Or psoriasis? The language was not totally clear, but the threat to the public health in a crowded city with no sewers was huge. Lepers were shunned, exiled to the desert. That was a common health practice until the bacillus that resembles tuberculosis was identified in 1874 and discovered to be less contagious than previously thought. In the days of Naaman, the disease was considered a curse from the gods, like modern people once viewed cancer and AIDS.

Imagine the kind of stress that drove the great man to accept the word of a captured slave girl, a word of hope spoken in the privacy of his wife's rooms. The girl told of the existence of a prophet in Israel, a worker of miracles who lived in the conquered land.

Life Challenges

Ultimately we are human, all of us, no matter our wealth or station, our job or

and grown spiritually. What happened to you when you learned about their diagnosis? How was your relationship with them affected?

Have you known people suffering into their last days whose friends simply deserted them or who were left to die alone? How different was it for you to walk that path with someone of courage and faith and to know when that person died, he or she was with God?

THE JOURNEY
❖ Using a Bible atlas, display the maps of Syria/Israel and chart a probable route for the general. How far did

name. When we are handed a terminal diagnosis, everything that has been our lifestyle is called into question. What was important to us shifts as our values shift. Whatever pride we had, whatever egoism or self-worth, all gets rocked to its foundation. If, in fact, this general truly had leprosy, what good would his wealth and position have been to him when his body became increasingly loathsome and he was forced to leave his home and family, cast out of society?

Twenty years ago I belonged to a small group of clergy who studied Scriptures together weekly. One of the Episcopal priests in that close group let us know he was experiencing symptoms he feared so greatly that he had not yet asked the medical profession for a diagnosis. We held him in prayer as he braved the medical tests—and came back with a diagnosis of ALS. They called it "Lou Gehrig's Disease." Having watched his father die that way, it was doubly hard for him, knowing what was coming into his life. Instead of hiding, he spent his final year of life doing everything he could to further care and research for those with ALS. He was truly a man of faith and courage whom I will never forget.

Beginning the Journey

In a state of desperate hope, the general drove with his chariot to the king's palace for any support possible. He shared the slave girl's words with his

22

he travel at each stage of the journey? About how long would it take to travel that distance on foot, carrying all the gifts?

Using a relief map, such as found in the Oxford Bible Atlas, make a diorama of the Holy Land and her neighbors that the whole education department of your church can use. Find a table or a piece of plywood you can put on legs and put a coat of waterproof urethane on it. Create the mountains and shapes of the coastlines with paper-maché or clay.

When those are dried, paint in the colors. Put in detail with the kinds of materials used for miniature model train landscapes.

❖ How different is the terrain from the terrain where you live? Find the rivers mentioned in the Scripture and look up a description of them in a Bible dictionary.

friend and king. These were oriental men in an oriental world of squalor and splendor who understood external power only.

Diplomatic immunity? Certainly. A letter to the king of Israel to command the healing of his valuable general? No problem.

Imagine the baggage train of so important a man: camels and mules loaded with talents of silver—10 of them. And shekels of gold—6,000 of them. In 1999, an Israeli shekel was valued at .2936 US dollars, which would be $1761.60. But real gold in the time of Naaman in an economy of trade and barter would have made the relative value enormously higher. They carried bales of finely woven fabrics from Damascus' finest tailors. Horses and chariots and servants, food and bedding and tents. How far from Damascus to Samaria? Forty miles? Fifty? A hundred?

See the maps of Syria/Lebanon and northern Israel. See the distance from the coastline to Damascus, a terrain that looks very familiar to a Californian. Coastal hills rise from a beachfront, dropping to the east in a long, fertile valley. The valley, which is the northern extension of the Great Rift Valley of Africa formed by the edge of the tectonic plate, is bounded on its eastern edge by the highest mountains in the area. Mount Hermon stands over 9200 feet, and the city of Damascus lies on its eastern slope rather like Reno and Carson City lie on the eastern face of the Sierra Nevada. From the slopes of Mount Hermon rise the headwaters of the Jordan, fed by tributaries as it finds its bed in the valley to the south, flowing through the Galilee and ending in the Dead Sea, another Death Valley lying hundreds of feet below sea level.

Naaman's train would have had to climb over the Golan Heights and down into northern Israel to find a place to ford the Jordan, then climb the West Bank into the ancient town of Samaria, seat of Israel's northern kingdom.

The king of Israel received General Naaman at his court, returned the amenities, opened the letter, and had an anxiety attack on the spot. This king was not a man of faith. He was a man of politics, and the political potential threw him into a defensive frenzy. He saw the impossibility rather than the possibility. As king of a petty, conquered state, he assumed the worst in what seemed a power game. He ripped his garments apart to display his grief.

We are not told how or when the word came to Elisha in his house that the king had been handed an impossible task. The "grapevine" worked very well. We are not told what Naaman and his traveling companions did in the interval. We are told only of Elisha's message to the king reminding him "that there is a prophet in Israel" (2 Kings 5:8). So the general and his entourage went to the house of the prophet—but did not meet him.

The first encounter—actually, non-encounter—between Naaman and Elisha was a study in culture shock and deliberate dislocation. We were shown

❖ Review what 2 Kings 5:5-7 says about the response of the king of Israel. The specific king is not identified; he may have been Ahaziah or Jehoram. Look up these two kings in a Bible dictionary to learn more about them and why it apparently did not occur to the king to send Naaman to Elisha.

❖ Read 2 Kings 2. What do you know about the personality of Elisha from those stories? Does he sound like your expectation of a "holy man"? How did those expectations of what it meant to be "holy" or to behave in a certain way that you might consider "holy" or "spiritual" change from his time to ours? Where do you think the changes came from?

❖ Discuss the impor-
tance of hospitality in
an arid climate. What
were the conse-
quences for that
society if hospitality
was not offered? What
might happen to a trav-
eler who could not
count upon finding at
least water or shelter
in a hostile climate?

rudeness and irascibility in 2 Kings 2. We have been told of the extravagant gift of "a double share of . . . spirit" (2 Kings 2:9) when Elijah left the earth, of miracles performed in the first moment when he took Elijah's cloak and parted the Jordan. We have also been told of his curse upon the boys who ridiculed his baldness. And so, at first, this appeared as just another instance of Elisha's arrogance. In the culturally accepted norm, this prophet who lived alone with one servant should have offered Naaman hospitality, or at least should have bowed to such an impor-tant man.

THE EYES OF GOD
❖ What experiences
have you had with the
exercises designed to
release your "left
brain"—your logical
mind? When have you
been able to "get out of
your head" and experi-
ence the world with
"the eyes of your
heart"? How was that
different for you?

Seeing With the Eyes of God

Look deeper. Look with the eyes of one who has been introduced to the *koans* of Zen training, the questions of the forest teachers, the curious responses of the Desert Fathers to their disciples. Look through the fine silk and woolen garments and the tattered flesh of the king's general and see the soul inside crying for wholeness.

The gifts of God demonstrated by the enigmatic Elisha should have made it possible for him to do the equivalent of "waving a magic wand" and sending Naaman home again with a whole hide. Instead Elisha ordered him, via his ser-vant's voice, to bathe in the Jordan seven times.

EXPECTATIONS
Together, create your own ritual of healing using prayer, litany, colors, candles, laying on of hands. What feels right? What happens to the group? Is the experience one you could use with some portion of your congregation?

❖ Reread 2 Kings 5:9-12. Journal for yourself an experience of a time when you tried to bargain with God. What was that about? What was at stake? What did you hope would happen? What actually happened? What did you learn from this experience?

Expectations

Naaman, having commanded his army in Israel, may have had some sense of the elaborate and expensive ritual healings detailed in Leviticus 14. He may have expected to use the silver and gold to pay for sacrificial animals, to shave all over, to wash his clothes, to be anointed with blood and oil. He may, in his desperate hope, have wanted all the drama of a magical rite. He did not even get a polite greeting.

Naaman's response was bluster and outrage. He did not get the welcome he thought he deserved. His bountiful treasures were rejected, unwanted. This "desert rat" was not even impressed with the fine garments he had brought! And that rejection left Naaman with no bargaining power, no leverage.

How many of us go to God assuming we have leverage? "Look God, after all I've done for you, you should heal my affliction, lift my depression, protect my child. I'll make you a deal."

No deal. Naaman was left standing at the doorway with no deal, just instructions to bathe in a free public river. No gold needed. The angry, frustrated general went away to sulk and, in his own way, panic.

How often have we carried baggage—loot, talents—that we hoped would buy us what our souls needed and discovered to our dismay that there was no rate of exchange with God?

26

**UNEXPECTED
SOURCES**

❖ Review the advice of the servants to Naaman in 2 Kings 5:1-3, 13. What did they risk to help their master? In this instance at least, the "underlings" had better sense than the powerful one. Have you been in a similar situation? If so, how did it feel to have clear insight into an issue that others could not see?

Have you ever been in Naaman's position—stuck in your assumptions or ego so that you could not immediately see what was right to do? If so, who helped you get unstuck?

In either instance, did you see the Spirit at work? If so, how?

❖ Consider Bishop Shamana's comments. In pairs, tell stories about some interaction with the Spirit. How did your faith grow or change in that interaction?

Learning From Unexpected Sources

Again, in the underlying threads of the story, Naaman's life was saved by the wisdom of a servant. The servants, who had witnessed the exchange at Elisha's door, may have known their master's pride and vulnerability better than anyone else did. One servant risked the pride and spoke to the reasonable man; he bypassed the "should" of a parent voice and side-stepped the upset feelings.

And there sat Naaman with talents and shekels around him, thinking of his wounded ego. He could not understand why he had come all this way just to be asked to bathe in a turgid, half-baked creek when the rivers of home were deeper and wider. The Amana River that ran clear from the Anti-Lebanon Mountains would have been a more magnificent tub. Naaman was a left-brained man seeing with half of his mind and therefore not seeing another potential.

Bishop Shamana, in *Seeing in the Dark* (Abingdon, 2001), reminds us that "healing and intercessory prayer are . . . methods that require a suspension of sequential linear logic" (page 71) and that "interaction with the Spirit will be disturbing, disorderly, surprising, even destabilizing" (page 86).

The general's servants were less hampered by success based on linear thinking, and so they challenged his mood with simple opportunity. How much easier to do what was asked? Shrugging, he complied.

The Rivers of Life

THE RIVERS OF LIFE

❖ What do you remember or what were you told about your baptism? Were you immersed? If so, what was that experience like? What did you think of it before or after? Compare your experience with that of others who were baptized by sprinkling or pouring.

Do a guided meditation for healing using this section of text, up to "His flesh was restored. . . ." Pause at the end of sentences or ideas to take time to reflect briefly on the scene and how you see yourself in it. Pay particular attention to what it "feels like" to be soaked in the cleansing water. Close the time of meditation with a minute or two of silence or quiet music.

❖ Tell stories of other biblical healings that have instructed you about the power of God. Read Mark 2:2-12. Imagine yourself as a participant in that scene. How would you see it? What do you

Imagine the rocky, muddy banks of the Jordan River. Imagine finding an accessible beach where there was a pool of water deep enough to bathe in, with the running current cleansing it. Bathing was not a constant in that culture. It took some decision and effort. For each of the seven times that Naaman walked into the river, his experience was different. From a wild hope for magic, his confronted mind had to shift to the situation at hand. He had been a realistic man, practical and competent, an important advisor to the king of Aram. It was a much longer journey than some fifty miles to a camp on the beach of a river. It was a longer way from a command in the desert to a bath in a stream. It was an immense journey from affairs of state to floating on his back in the sunshine of a warm pool.

Along with the dry, itchy skin, things got washed downstream that he had never thought about before: things like the weight of maintaining an image of health instead of the joy of health itself, like the stress of command instead of accepting guidance into simpler ways from his own servants, like leaving off heavy robes of state or armor to swim light as a leaf in the water, moving from crowds and cities and armies to blessed solitude, moving from the darkness of a goat hair tent into the light made by God. *Made by God.* How could he not get in touch with the floating motions of his own body without noticing how amazing that body was? And how amazing would be God who could make such a body?

28

think happened there? How do these experiences help you get in touch with the awesome healing power of God?

❖ What would it mean to you today to be able to "wash away" all the guilt and stress of your own life? What would it mean to you to be "clean" in the biblical sense? How might you live differently in the world?

THE COURAGE TO ASK
Do an exercise of Appreciative Inquiry with your group. Form pairs and take turns interviewing one another. Be prepared (take notes if you want) to introduce your partner to the group when you return. Take at least twenty minutes of uninterrupted time for each person.

What have been the highlights of your faith journey? Where have you seen your faith at its most powerful? How

Imagine that with the layers of skin that washed away, layers of guilt and stress and ego washed downstream. Years of grief and the responsibility of sending men to their deaths floated away. The man who rose from the river for the seventh time was not the same man who entered the first time. "His flesh was restored like the flesh of a young boy, and he was clean" (2 Kings 5:14). In some ways he was like the young slave who had urged him to seek Elisha at the outset.

Clean in Israel was not just washed. "Wash me, and I shall be whiter than snow," wrote the psalmist (Psalm 51:7b). *Clean* meant forgiven, healed, whole, restored to purity. God's incredible gift to a worldly, bloodstained man. Even he . . . *clean.*

The Courage to Ask

When Naaman and his group returned to the prophet, there was a different dynamic from a changed man. Arrogance and pride gave way to gratitude and commitment. "Now I know," he said (2 Kings 5:15; see also 1 Corinthians13:12). Instead of buying his healing as a right, an expectation of power, Naaman wanted to make a gift to the prophet who had showed him the way to God. But Elisha wanted no part of the silver and gold (2 Kings 5:15-16). He knew whom he served; and he knew too, I think, how little it cost him to point the way. Consistent with biblical stories of

have you been able to help someone in a place where healing was needed? What have been the greatest gifts that a faith community has brought into your life? What are the gifts that you bring to this faith community?

After the interviews are complete, gather in double-pairs or in the whole group, if it is not too big, and briefly introduce your partner using your new knowledge of that person. When each one has had a chance to do so, share the surprises that you experienced in learning about a person you may have thought you knew.

healing, the healing was never only for the "in-group" but for neighbors as well, believers or not, who had the courage to ask.

When we talk about healing, we must talk about how it is different from cure. There is medicine and surgery for cure. Only God heals. We have seen miracles where both happened or sadness where neither happened. It is harder for people without faith to recognize a healing where there may not have been a cure, but it happens. In my years of working with people living with HIV, I witnessed every variation. There were people whose bodies died from AIDS but whose souls gained light and beauty as they moved into relationship with God and walked through that gateway.

Naaman tried again to give the prophet a gift of gold, but he did not insist. Along with his healing came a new recognition of the value of the world's goods in the face of the simplicity of God. And Naaman was committing his life of faith to this powerful God, the God of these people he himself had conquered with his army. Wanting something tangible as a reminder, Naaman asked for two mule-loads of dirt. And he asked for one more indulgence.

Knowing he was going home to his king and the life of a courtier, he asked prior pardon for having to go through the motions of accepted worship practices in the society to which he returned (2 Kings 5:17-18). The court of Aram worshiped Rimmon, or Ramman in the Akkadian language. He was the ancient god of

30

❖ Brainstorm together about what our world might look like if we could move to that place of "Go in peace." At URI we call them "cultures of peace." What would your community look like if it perceived itself as a culture of peace?

A CHANGE OF SPIRIT
Look again at 2 Kings 5:15-19a. Note the changes in Naaman's demeanor and note his attitude about profiting from God's grace. How were Naaman and Elisha relating to each other at this point? How was it different from their first encounter?

❖ What is it that signifies for you that "there is no God in all the earth except in Israel"?

Using modeling clay or other art supplies, fashion what for you would be the "two mule-loads of earth"—something that will represent or signify the presence and power of God.

thunder and storm, also identified with the Roman god Jupiter. The prophet answered, "Go in peace" (5:19).

How different an understanding here from the story in the New Testament of the rich young man (Matthew 19:16-22). Elisha was clear that this man would not move to Israel and live under Levitical law. What he observed was the change of heart; and as a prophet of God, he was willing to let God's plan evolve for Naaman in its own way.

A Change of Spirit

When we met Naaman, he was presented as a powerful, decisive, worldly man of action and resolve. As we came to see him in his interaction with Elisha, we noticed his naive, vulnerable side. After pouting about his slight by Elisha and the silly course of action prescribed by the prophet, Naaman—at the urging of underlings—complied. When he experienced his healing and a religious turnaround, it was innocent and shallow; but it was a beginning that no doubt pleased God.

In Naaman's understanding that "there is no God in all the earth except in Israel" (2 Kings 5:15), he also naively assumed that "the earth" was somehow necessary for the worship of this God—thus, his request for enough dirt to carry home to create a "mini-Israel" for the worship of this wonderful God (5:17). Naaman's earnest, but uncritical, theological stance may seem inadequate to us when we realize the total commitment God requires of us. We may be impatient with Naaman's immediate distraction from this newfound faith, but Elisha did not judge him harshly—a lesson to us, to be sure.

The Rest of the Story

Elisha's response to Naaman was gracious. In stark contrast, Gehazi, the servant of Elisha, was disdainful. Perhaps Gehazi felt that this conquering general did not deserve what he received from God at Elisha's hand. Perhaps Gehazi felt that some price must be exacted to satisfy the great gift Naaman had been given. Perhaps he simply saw an opportunity, however dishonest and unethical, and could not resist trying to seize it.

Whatever his motivation, Gehazi ran after Naaman to squeeze something from him; and Naaman, not realizing that he was being taken, gladly handed over what Gehazi asked (2 Kings 5:19b-24). Gehazi no doubt was pleased with his coup, but one lie led to another until he found himself in great peril (5:25-27). He spent the remainder of his days with the disgrace, pain, and ignominy of his community-shattering disease. What had been healed in Naaman was taken on by the faithless, devious servant.

What are we to learn from this dreadful twist of fate and future to Gehazi and to his "descendants forever" (2 Kings 5:27)? This action must be considered in the midst of all the other undulations of our sometimes brave, sometimes broken, humanity?

❖ Close with prayer for persons who are broken by disease or impure motives. Give thanks for the healers and other faithful persons whose grace extends to all.

the story: the expectation of the Syrian king contrasted with the panic of the king of Israel; the ease of healing against Naaman's assumption that he must fight and conquer to obtain; the instrument of God's healing in someone rude and abrupt rather than polished and politically correct; the faithfulness and allegiance of the servants of the "pagan" Naaman (including his Israelite slave) against the treachery of the prophet's servant; Naaman's expectation that the God of the universe is tied to a clump of dirt; the Israelite expectation that God only favors one nation over God's grace to all nations.

Who is this God of reversals? Who is this God of unexpected healing? Who is this God who includes all and not just some? As our world moves from a place of blame, arrogance, unchecked assumptions, and exploitation to dealing with people as God's precious creations, we will better understand and appreciate the mystery of a God who tells the one we least expect, "Go in peace."

Chapter Three

The Power of Trust
Mark 4:35-41

PURPOSE
To look at the ways in which our faith works in our lives and during the times of storm.

THE SESSION PLAN
Choose from among the core teaching activities (identified with ❖) and add options in *bold italics* to extend beyond a 45-60 minute session.

THE DILEMMA
❖ Read Mark 4:35-41. Then close your eyes and imagine what it might have been like for you to be in that boat during the storm. What might you have done? To which of the characters in the story do you feel closest?

Some went down to the sea in ships,
    doing business on the mighty waters;
they saw the deeds of the LORD,
    his wondrous works in the deep.
For he commanded and raised the stormy wind,
    which lifted up the waves of the sea.
They mounted up to heaven, they went down to the depths;
    their courage melted away in their calamity.
        (Psalm 107:23-26)

The Dilemma

Seasick and out of control. Afraid. The psalm was penned centuries before the story told in Mark's Gospel took place. When we find ourselves in the grip of creation's raw power, we have no bargaining power, no leverage. History is filled with stories of people caught in storms at sea who promised God all sorts of things, from building a church to repentance of sin, if only they could live. Those who were saved from the sea told tales of God's mercy and wonder. Those who were not, never came home. Everyone has known stories of the sea's fury.

It had been a busy day. There were large crowds gathered at the shore, so many that few people could see or hear the wondrous rabbi they had come to see. In order to create a little distance from which to speak, Jesus got into one of the fishing boats near the shore. While someone rowed to keep the boat stable, he balanced himself on a pair of uneven struts so that his weight would not capsize the boat. While his body worked to keep its balance in the choppy surf of the lake's movement toward the shore, he focused his speaking voice and told parables for hours. The afternoon went by with Jesus explaining stories to the people and to his companions. As the sun sank in the west and the crowd dispersed to their homes and cook fires, a tired and hungry teacher asked to be taken across the lake to get away from it all. On the rocking motion of the lake, he fell fast asleep upon the stern bench.

The Discovery

In 1986 two brothers, Yuval and Moshe Lufan, who lived by the shores of Lake Kinneret, took advantage of the drought-lowered surface to search for artifacts from earlier times. A cache of newly exposed coins in the sand and mud alerted them to look deeper for the source of such a treasure. Off the shore they noticed an outline that seemed to be boat-shaped, something deeply buried in the mud and clay near Migdal (Magdala). In so warm a freshwater lake, wooden

learned to apply that creativity to the tools and conveyances that make our lives abundant?

artifacts rarely survived. The archaeologists who came and probed the shape discovered an ancient boat made in a style used only from about 2000 B.C. to the end of the Roman occupation. Mortise and tenon joints were the first clue. Iron nails in the upper strake were evidence that the boat could not pre-date the Iron Age (beginning about 800 B.C.). Also found with the boat were a terra cotta lamp and clay cooking pot consistent with items used from about 100 B.C. to A.D. 100.

The boat measured 27 feet by 7.6 feet and was made of and mended with several different types of wood. It was designed for both sail and oar. Carbon 14 testing placed it at 70 B.C. +/- 90 years. With careful hands, it was cradled and carried to the museum at Ginosar. If it was not precisely the boat that Jesus knew, it was very similar.

JESUS CONNECTION
❖ Use a concordance and find other references to boats and the sea. How have the authors of the various books of the Bible used the ocean or journeys by boat to illustrate a spiritual experience? Why is one of the key symbols of the church a ship?

The Jesus Connection

Aside from the interest of the boat builders in such a find, much interest was focused on the fact that this first-century B.C. boat preserved in the clay and mud shed light upon the style of boats plying the Sea of Galilee in Jesus' day. Jesus made several references in the Gospels that demonstrated his awareness of nautical lore. For those who are fascinated with the details of Jesus' life and world, this boat might be of interest. It was the first and only example found of the boats of his era, and it gives us a picture of

Remember the sailors.
During a time of class prayer, sing "Eternal Father, Strong to Save" and pray for those on the seas of the world.

❖ Refer to Psalm 107:23-26 and write your own psalm for a time of calamity. How would you characterize your own experience and God's involvement in it? How would you offer complaints, pleas, or thanksgiving in your psalm? How do you believe God would, or did, answer?

ABANDONED
❖ Read and compare the accounts in Matthew (8:23-27), Mark (4:35-41), and Luke (8:22-25). The differences are subtle. What are the major "movements" in the story? How do they differ? Do these differences really make a difference? If so, how? What is the most important point of this story for you?

what the boat might have looked like in this scene from Mark.

Twenty-seven feet was a fine size for a day-sailer, but in a sudden squall it would not seem very big at all. The low sides that allowed for fishing also allowed the waves to wash aboard. Cut-out bleach bottles were not available for bailers then. In a few verses Mark painted the picture: a small boat, a sleeping teacher, several frightened fishermen whose "courage melted away in their calamity" (Psalm 107:26).

These were not landlubbers who were out of their element. These were grown men familiar with their craft, working fishermen who knew the waters of the lake well. What made the situation worse for them was that Jesus, in his exhaustion, was not present. He was not awake to share their fear.

Abandoned to Fate

Where is God? Doesn't God care what happens to us? Our faith will shrink if we believe that God cares nothing for the fear and pain in our lives. Our human relationships cannot survive in the face of the other's lack of concern. *"Don't you care?"*

Matthew's version of this story (Matthew 8:23-27) added another dimension of possible reference to the lack of faith of the disciples as they set out for the other shore. Matthew emphasizes that the disciples willingly followed Jesus into the boat, which for this Gospel

Search your hymnal for songs about courage or salvation. Sing or say some of them together. How do they inspire you to withstand the storms of life? crises of faith? How do they remind you of Jesus' presence in time of need? When you are experiencing trouble, do you ever find a particular hymn "in your head"? If so, how has that helped you?

❖ Have there been times when God seemed suddenly distant? If "distance" is your typical feeling about the presence of God, how might you overcome that to be aware of God's nearness to you?

writer is a metaphor for the church. Rather than functioning as a "nature miracle" for Matthew, this story reflects the experience of the early church—willing disciples called and faithful but also buffeted by dreadful storms of persecution and discouragement. The disciples' cry in Mark, "Do you not care that we are perishing?" (Mark 4:38) is replaced with the reference to their salvation history, "Lord save us! We are perishing!" (Matthew 8:25).

All the Synoptic Gospel accounts, including Luke's (Luke 8:22-25), focus on the fact that the disciples were still not sure who Jesus was. We can, from our vantage of certainty that Jesus is the divine Son, assume that he would not lose his life to the storm; but the disciples' use of "we" and "us" probably included him. They were clearly terrified of drowning in the harsh sea along with their master.

Jesus' peaceful sleeping might have made more sense to the men if they had the least insight into Jesus' grasp of the cosmic timing of things. The man who had an innate intuition of the timing of his own call, of his own place in God's plan for him, knew it was not his time to die. Whatever happened with that storm was temporary if uncomfortable. There was no reason for him to be afraid.

The men waited out of respect for Jesus as long as they could stand it. And then the child-panic overwhelmed them; and they woke him out of that deep sleep with their cries: "Teacher, do you not care that we are perishing?" (Mark 4:38).

38

There is something distinctive here about the way the disciples addressed Jesus. The insiders never called Jesus "teacher." They called him "Lord." (See Matthew 8:25.) Only outsiders called him "teacher." Here in Mark the men suddenly responded as if he were a stranger. There was a sudden shift, a distance between them.

The Stranger Among Them

Jesus' waking response was even stranger. Instead of helping to bail or grabbing a line to steady the boat, he turned not in an attitude of begging prayer but in a curt voice of authority and spoke to the sky itself: "Peace! Be still!" (Mark 4:39). And it was.

Imagine the expressions on the faces of those men at that moment. Watch them looking at their feet ankle-deep in water, at the horizon suddenly flat, at each other in shock. And, finally, together, at Jesus. Who was this man? Was he a man at all? The picture of Jesus sleeping in the stern of the boat may have reminded his companions of the prophet Jonah (Jonah 1:5-6); but Jonah was a mortal who could also have drowned with the fearful, Tarshish-bound mariners.

Jewish lore is replete with stories of rabbis and teachers, stern scholars or joyous, thoughtful mystics or explicators of Scripture, who lightened their lessons with wordless songs. There were stories of teachings and healings and faith, but there was never a rabbi like this. The

THE STRANGER

❖ Journal your own experience of a relationship that shifted from what you thought it was to something else. Very often after a divorce, for example, the partners will say that the former wife/husband "was not who I thought she/he was." What do you think happened in your own "shift"? What made you realize the difference in the other person or the difference in the foundations of the relationship?

❖ If the class is a "safe space," share these findings in a discussion. How does your understanding of your own experience change how you view this shift of relationship between the disciples and Jesus?

Have a local rabbi talk about the tradition of teachers/disciples in Judaism and share some "wordless songs" with the class.

Note Pheme Perkins' comment about Near Eastern mythology and the conclusions the disciples could draw about "Who is this?" Suppose that in addition to what you know of God, you had to draw on what you know of mythology (or science fiction or childhood hero stories) to help you as a disciple in that boat. Imagine what stories, heroes, or other images would come to mind. How would you answer the question, "Who then is this?" Would the answer assuage your fear? Why or why not?

only parallel tales from history were stories of the gods from the ancient world. Says theologian Pheme Perkins in *The New Interpreter's Bible* (Abingdon, 1995, Volume VIII, page 580), "Ancient Near Eastern mythology depicted the storm god triumphing over the raging waters of the monster of chaos (e.g. Baal vs. Yam; Marduk vs. Tiamat). . . . The mythological and poetic imagery of God triumphing over the raging waters makes clear the response to the final question, 'Who then is this. . .?' "

Awe, the root of the word *awful* or *awesome:* in a new way—utterly different. Jesus was suddenly someone apart, isolated from the norm. And what did this awesome teacher/god say to the disciples? What's your problem? "Why are you afraid? Have you still no faith?" (Mark 4:40). Underneath that remark, we may also hear the unspoken sigh, "after all the time I have spent with you." This was a moment when the dissociation between the man and the Messiah began to widen in the minds of the fishermen.

THE FAITH QUESTION
Using a Bible atlas, find pictures of the Sea of Galilee and learn more about it. Imagine yourself on a stormy lake, 4 miles from the nearest shore, with 150 feet of water beneath you and just the hull of a 27-foot boat separating you

The Faith Question

To be fair, fishermen in a storm-tossed boat about to sink were not thinking about faith at all. The Sea of Galilee was a beautiful but dangerous body of water. With a maximum depth of 150 feet and a width of 8 miles, it was not the place for a swim on a stormy evening! The surrounding hills, at about 1200-1500 feet, caused occasional abrupt changes in

from the depths. Can you swim that far in rain and waves? What might you have been thinking in such a situation?

❖ Journal or tell the stories that have been central to your trust in God. What has been your experience of being pulled out of the "dailyness" of life by a call to see God's hand in the plan for some- one's life, including yours?

❖ With one or two partners or in your journal, discuss or write about when you are most likely to think about faith. Do you

temperature on this below-sea-level lake, which in turn produced sudden and violent storms. Unprotected parts of the lake were also subject to hard winds— good for sailing, but perilous as well.

With this well-known geography les- son in mind, the disciples were more probably thinking about drowning! Or they were thinking about losing a boat they could not afford to replace or about the probability of their families starving without Dad to make a living.

We do it a lot, don't we? We get caught up in the drama of our lives—the disobe- dience of our kids, the tragedy of a friend's terminal diagnosis, the news of an associate's upcoming wedding. We get buried in the "dailyness" of our lives—up at dawn, off to work, home at dark facing chores or housework to be done. We go through the motions, try to get to church on Sunday, try to get to the grocery store on the way home to make sure there will be enough lunches for the week. We drop by the dry cleaners, pick up a neighbor's child too. We stuff laun- dry into the machine while we make din- ner and talk on the phone. Do we think about faith?

More likely, we think about faith when we are sitting in the funeral home stunned at the death of a friend. Blew an aneurysm at fifty and drove into the porch of the house down the street. Breast cancer at forty-four and left three children behind. Or more horrifying, the public memorial service for a seven- year-old girl kidnapped, raped, and mur- dered by a neighborhood man. Victims of

ever think that God's "back is turned" or that God is "asleep at the switch" and thus not paying attention? Have you ever asked God, "Don't you care?" If so, describe that experience? What, if anything, resolved it?

a terrorist's bomb in Oklahoma City. Young American sailors blown to pieces while their ship was docked in a foreign port. The events of September 11, 2001. Where was God? Asleep?

There is a Jewish tale about the universe being so big that God could not keep an eye on everything at once, and thus God's back was turned sometimes. Some Jews explain the Holocaust this way.

Don't you care? How is it possible to have faith in a God who does not seem to be there when we think God should be? How can we understand a God who lets the storms in our lives happen to us? What does it mean to trust?

THE FEAR FACTOR
❖ Why do you suppose fear is so deeply "hardwired" into the human psyche? How does Jesus' question, "Why are you afraid" strike you? Would there be any reason to think that even the most faithful person would not be afraid in the midst of such a terrible storm? Does showing fear connote to you a lack of faith? Explain your answer.

The Fear Factor

It is possible there may be a clue in that irate waking response of Jesus to the sailors: "Why are you afraid?" So much of our life, if we are honest with our inner self, is constructed around fear. We work overtime to put money away "just in case." We pay thousands of dollars every year for insurance of various kinds. We stock food in order to be prepared for emergencies. And we do everything we can think of to protect our own life.

One of my neighbors went overboard during the Y2K panic and stocked his garage (We do not have basements in California.) with a generator, food, water, and flashlights. He was livid that I was not worried. When the New Year 2000 came, we discovered that the only Y2K problem we had was a VCR that could no longer be programmed to record. It was waiting for a date in 1900

If the gift of true faith is the promise of resurrection in Christ, why are we so afraid? Why do we work so hard to protect these lives we cannot possibly lose?

There was a woman in one of the churches I served who taught me the lesson of death. She was one of those quiet people whose name I barely remembered until she wound up in the hospital. For two years she fought for her life in the face of a missed diagnosis. What the physicians dismissed as a bleeding stomach ulcer resistant to medication was belatedly found to be a gaping hole in the esophagus that bled continually into the body cavities. When the pain was bad, she said to me, "Jesus suffered for me. I can suffer for him."

I went home and punched the door frame in the parsonage in my rage that this sweet and faithful woman should go through such agony. During the two weeks she was in a coma, I went to the ICU and read psalms to her while the nurses looked at me sideways. Days later I walked into the hospital and found her sitting up in a ward. "I heard you," she said. "I recognized your voice." I was stunned.

But it got worse. Finally the family called me one night. When I arrived, she was tossing and turning in her bed, literally fighting for her life. They left me with her, and I watched in silence for a while. And I said, "Stop. I can't stand it any more." And she stopped. She lay still in the bed and held my hand, and we

❖ Consider the story of the author's pastoral experience with the parishioner who died from the consequences of the esophageal disease. What are the troubling aspects of this story? the touching ones? the surprising ones?

Then consider the questions near the top of this page: If the gift of faith is resurrection, why are we afraid?

❖ How does this woman's willingness to suffer for the Christ who suffered for her engage your faith?

Play a tape or CD of the music of Taizé. Sing or hum along with the music. (You can also get samples from their website at www.taise.fr.) Close your eyes if you wish; during the musical petitions, think about your fears. Lay them before God. Do not attempt to pray in words; just rest in God's Spirit.

prayed together. We talked for a while. She was calm and peaceful and smiling when I left her. Within hours she was gone. Some of the silk roses from her memorial service were used in my bridal bouquet. I have them still.

In the darkest moments of fear,
  the storms of my life,
  the creaking shudders of my mental
    nutshell upon the deeps,
  be the Word that stills,
  that lights, that heals.
This fragile craft that carries my soul
springs leaks in the stresses of life.
Be the caulk that holds me together.
Be the wind in my sails that blows me
where You would have me serve.
Still the waves that threaten to swamp
my mind until only a gentle rocking
lets me rest in God.
  Jesus, be the Word that calms.

CARRYING FAITH FORWARD
Coordinate a get-together with your interfaith neighbors and share some Appreciative Inquiry time with them. Use the pattern of Appreciative Inquiry from Chapter Two, pairing off for personal interviews, then introducing your new friend to a small group. Bring the whole group back together and talk about community issues that concern all of you. Then take the process

Carrying Faith Forward

"Have you still no faith?" Walking as I do these days in the excitement of interfaith cooperation, the concept of faith has become wider and deeper for me. Sharing discussions and worship with Buddhists and Sikhs and Hindus and Sufis has made a better Christian of me. It is not the faith that clings in fear to walls that divide and separate the faith traditions. It is the deeply rooted faith in God that lets me honor these people who are faithful in their own traditions. There is so much to be learned from them. Everything that deepens my understand-

one step further: Dream together how the future might be better. Have someone record the ideas/dreams on a flipchart with markers.

Notice how many ways your needs for your community are alike. In what ways might these needs be different? How might you work together to begin to make the dreams come true?

Find a copy of What's My Type? by Hurley and Dobson. Copy the questions that allow you to choose which numbers might apply to you. Browse the series of questions for the types and see which one(s) seems to describe you best. Discuss what insights come from the personality types for you. If you want to go deeper, continue with the process of learning about "wings" and "arrows" to help you better discover your own spiritual path.

❖ What "masks" have your worn to protect yourself in public? Do they work now? Do you need them? Have they

ing of God deepens my commitment to life and erases my fear of death. Just as that dear, faithful woman taught me so long ago, we shall live again.

What Jesus was saying in his newly awakened, short-tempered way was, "The storm cannot hurt you; life cannot destroy your soul. Only your own fear can do that." Remember Paul's statement of faith in Romans 8:38-39: "For I am convinced that neither death, nor life, nor angels, nor rulers, nor things present, nor things to come, nor powers, nor height, nor depth, nor anything else in all creation, will be able to separate us from the love of God in Christ Jesus our Lord."

Part of my education for Spiritual Direction included study of the Enneagram, a tool for understanding one's personal traits and motivators. It is an ancient practice of spiritual maturity that was brought into this country about thirty years ago and has become very popular. Based on a mathematical sum, it allows us to perceive people as nine major types that each has "wings" and "arrows" of growth and stress. The Enneagram helps us to recognize what drives our life scripts and the goals towards which we need to reach.

Dozens of books on the Enneagram are available now. It has been a valuable tool in my own journey. One of its insights, though not unique to the Enneagram, is that we are motivated at our most secret levels by one of three basic functions: anger, fear, or the need for love. We live out one of these drives without necessarily knowing it. It is not

become a handicap? What might you need to let go of or to change? What instances can you recall from the Bible about times when Jesus as a teacher was able to show someone a clue to his or her own spiritual growth and understanding?

❖ How has the God who calms the storms become your God? Who do you think this is?

CLOSE

❖ As part of a time of prayer and worship, light a candle in honor of the ones who have been "lights" in your journey of faith. Tell the stories of why these particular people have been so important to you. How did they come into your life? How did they awaken your faith? Put the candles onto a table in the center of the circle or against the wall that is central to your worship or class time. Offer prayers for these "lights" and then together say the prayer on page 44 that begins, "In the darkest moments . . ."

until we recognize and acknowledge that center that we can begin to loosen its hold upon our unconscious reactions. Only self-observation will reveal which center is our own. Only when we accept that drive can we unhook its hold upon our lives.

Clearly the disciples, at least at that moment on the lake, were motivated by fear, though anger and love may have held some sway, if they believed that the master who claimed to love them was unfazed by their evident peril.

Who is this man Jesus? If he is the God who could calm the storm, how much simpler for him to see into our hearts, our minds, our fears? What is this faith God wants us to have? Is it as simple as trusting in the life God gave us? as relying on the strength of the Master?

O LORD, how manifold are your works!. . .
Yonder is the sea, great and wide. . . .
There go the ships,
    and Leviathan that you formed to
      sport in it.
           (Psalm 104:24-26).

Chapter Four

The Power of Resurrection
John 20:1-18

PURPOSE
The purpose of this session is to explore resurrection as a new relationship, then and now.

THE SESSION PLAN
Choose from among the core teaching activities (identified with ❖) and add options in ***bold italics*** to extend beyond a 45-60 minute session.

ON THAT MORNING
❖ Read John 20:1-18 together. Put yourself into the story in a new way. Imagine what it might have been like to be Mary Magdalene or to be Jesus. Try to imagine yourself as someone of a different gender. What might have gone on inside this person that the story does not describe? How does the exercise deepen your under-

On That Morning

A couple of days have gone by since the ghastly, earth-shattering scene on Friday. Those who heard about it have sat stunned or have passed on the news to others. Those who saw it have done little but weep; pray; or ask in hushed tones what on earth happened to their dreams, their friend, their hero, their lives. Some were afraid. If Jesus were a criminal, who would be looking for them next?

No one wanted much to eat. The women tried to go through the motions of daily life, but the bread was salted with tears and mostly left uneaten. The men sat shoulder to shoulder, saying little.

With that womanly need to take care of someone, Mary from Migdal, who had traveled with the band since her own healing and whose money had helped to support the group (Luke 8:2-3), picked up the necessary ingredients and took off down the hill. Frankincense and myrrh— a noble's gift at Jesus' birth in anticipation of a noble end. Instead, there was a miserable death on a convict's cross and

47

*Map the ancient
Frankincense Trail
through southern
Arabia.* (Use a Bible
atlas, such as the
Oxford Bible Atlas, to
find the route and a
Bible dictionary to look
up frankincense.)
Sheba is on the south-
ern tip of Arabia, per-
haps 1400 miles from
Jerusalem. What is
frankincense? Why
was it worth more than
gold? Why would
someone use this sub-
stance as part of the
ceremonies of death?

❖ Read the parallel
Gospel accounts in
Luke 24, Matthew 28,
and Mark 16. How are
the stories different?
Which version seems
most possibly true to
you? You can do this
as a journaling exer-
cise or as a group
discussion.

*On a map of
Jerusalem, find the
garden.* If anyone has
been there on a trip,
have this person tell
what it is like today.

**THE HERITAGE
AS DRAMA**
❖ What is it like to
have someone sud-
denly missing?

a chilly burial in a borrowed cave of a tomb.

Having listened to all the paranoid ones wondering about their possibly being pursued and grieving deeply for the loss of her mentor and friend, she was hardly in an emotional state to stick calmly to observed reality. Bad enough to be on the errand she undertook without finding what she found. Not only was there no body to care for, there was only an empty tomb with the stone rolled away.

Luke gave Mary the company of several women (Luke 23:55–24:3). Matthew gave her one companion—another Mary (Matthew 28:1). Mark gave her a third companion—Salome (Mark 16:1). All the Gospel versions of this story run in different directions and give differing accounts of the action.

John's version of the scene left Mary Magdalene utterly alone in the dark before dawn at the entrance to the empty tomb, and her sudden reaction to the secondary loss of Jesus' body put her into instant motion. Running. Running back up the hill, the stairs, into the room, stumbling over long skirts, breathless with running and panic: He's gone! "They have taken the Lord out of the tomb" (John 20:2b).

The Heritage as Drama

Because of the vivid telling of these stories of the death and loss, the subsequent action of the various people, and the centrality of the story to the Christian faith,

❖ How has your church used drama to teach Scripture?

Nearly all churches of all denominations have some kind of Christmas play that the children do for them. How might the adults in your church partake of this kind of dramatic teaching element? In medieval times, the plays were given on the church steps in the town square. These plays were a particularly important Christian education tool when most people were illiterate. Different guilds had their own scripts and competed to see whose was the best or the funniest. Here is an opportunity to try a brief and ancient form. Use the script to the right to act out the *Quem Quaeritis*. Rewrite it for use in an Easter worship service at your church.

these were the first scenes to be dramatized in the church. The earliest written modern drama was a script for an Easter trope entitled *Quem Quaeritis,* based on these tales, to be produced as part of a tenth-century worship service. It was considered the beginning of modern theatre. As the church realized the powerful aspect of drama and music, the use of both grew and grew over the next several centuries. Plays were written for every feast day, and there were productions put on by the various guilds in the cities to tell the stories in and around the Gospels as they came alive for the people of that day.

The *Quem Quaeritis* Trope

From the introit of the Mass at Easter found in a tenth-century manuscript in the monastery at Saint Gall.

INTERROGATIO. *Quem quaeritis in sepulchro, O Christicolae?*

RESPONSIO. *Jesum Nazarenum crucifixum, o caelicolae.*

ANGELI. *Non est hic; surrexit, sicut praedixierat. Ite, nuntiate quia surrexit de sepulchro.*

Question [by the ANGELS]. Whom do ye seek in the sepulcher, O followers of Christ?

Answer [by the MARYS]. Jesus of Nazareth, who was crucified, just as he foretold.

The ANGELS. *He is not here: he is risen, just as he foretold. Go, announce that he is risen from the sepulcher.*
(*Medieval and Tudor Drama,* edited by John Gassner, Bantam books, 1963, page 35)

AT THE EMPTY TOMB

❖ Based on all the reading you have done, who do you think this "beloved disciple" might have been? (See John 20:1-2 and John 11:35-44.)

Use a Bible concordance to look up other references to "the disciple whom Jesus loved" and to Lazarus and activity at Bethany.

❖ Why do you think the Gospel never names the beloved disciple? As you try to guess his identity, how does that change the story for you?

❖ Reread John 20:3-10. What happens here? Form small groups of three or four. Imagine that you came to the place where you expected to see a loved one either laid out or interred and the body was gone. Think about what you believe about resurrection. (Remember John 20:9.) Imagine your response there and after you returned to your home. What did you do? How like that of the disciples might your own understanding be? Take turns telling the rest of that story.

At the Empty Tomb

Running. Two disciples took off running. Peter ran; but the other disciple, "the one whom Jesus loved," typically understood to be the Gospel writer John, impelled by that love, got there first—and stopped at the entrance to the tomb (John 20:2-5). Some traditions think this man might have been Lazarus. If so, he had no need to inspect the inside of a tomb. He had been there before.

Peter went in. Dear Peter, who rushed ahead so many times and understood only later; Peter, who had to be shown. Peter went to see for himself, to see the place, to see the linen wrappings. As usual, Peter did not "get it"; and he went away. The other disciple, with insight born of intimacy, "also went in, and he saw and believed" (John 20:6-8), not only that the tomb was empty but also that the absence of Jesus' body signified Jesus' conquest of death. If this disciple whom Jesus loved was Lazarus, then who better to have been able to grasp the ultimate possibility. Lazarus had been raised from his own tomb by the word and power of Jesus (John 11:35-44). Lazarus had staggered from his own tomb still bound in death's shroud. If Lazarus was the other man at the empty tomb, he saw the cloth left behind by a man dead no more, bound no more. He had no idea how, but he could believe in the possibility.

50

The Resurrection Enigma

The how of the Resurrection has exercised minds for two millennia, and that exercise has yielded every response from skepticism to belief. One possible explanation came out of the detailed and determined research done on what is evidently an ancient burial cloth. Ian Wilson in his book *The Shroud of Turin* (Image Books, 1979) tracked all the scientific research and the long curious history of the linen shroud. With the establishment of Carbon 14 dating, weaving technique, and pollen analysis, the cloth was determined to have matched the time and place of Jesus' death. Scientific study of the facial detail and imprint on the surface of the cloth through spectroscopy and the elimination of the idea of a scorch marking among the spots of blood and fluid absorbed into the fibers left scientists at Albuquerque—not far from Alamagordo, New Mexico, where the first atomic bomb was tested—with the idea of a thermonuclear flash so brief that the fibers were not damaged. Another chemist referred to it as "flash photolysis."

Wilson hypothesizes, "In the darkness of the Jerusalem tomb the dead body of Jesus lay, unwashed, covered in blood, on a stone slab. Suddenly, there is a burst of mysterious power from it. In that instant the blood dematerializes, dissolved perhaps by the flash, while its image and that of the body becomes indelibly fused onto the cloth, preserving for posterity a literal 'snapshot' of the

51

❖ Losing someone who has been impor-

❖ Losing someone who has been important to us is one of the deepest kinds of pain we humans can experience. Share a time of prayer for those in grief and loss. Send them a card or note to let them know they are not alone.

Resurrection" (page 251). The scientific and theological juries are still out on this subject, but it is tantalizing. As we noticed in Chapter One of this study, here is the tension between faith and science again.

Whatever happened in that dark tomb, whatever energy was poured into the man or came from him, we are still fascinated by the mystery. In some ways, we have been so busy with our fascination regarding "how" that we may have spent less time wondering about the vital question of "why." Why would the Son of Man—the Son of God—allow the death in the first place if not to tell us something critical about the relationship between life and death itself?

LEFT ALONE

❖ Read John 20:11-18. Close your eyes and try to imagine the scene and how you think Mary might have been feeling. Have one person read this first paragraph (through "more attached to Jesus than anyone else?") as a guided meditation. Read it slowly, pausing after each movement of the story so that others can absorb the scene. Try to be aware of what you might feel, see, smell, and hear.

After the last sentence, remain with your eyes closed until you feel like opening them.

Left Alone

Peter dealt with his own level of evidence—and went home. The other disciple, perhaps more thoughtfully, did the same. And there, abandoned to her task, was Mary, alone, with nothing left to do but weep. Face awash, eyesight blurred, she moved towards the only comfort left: the place where Jesus had been. If there was no more to this tale, she might have sat on the cave's shelf grasping the linen wrappings and cried herself dry. In that moment, she had lost everything: friend, beloved, mentor, healer, and the hope of the nation to lift the Roman oppression. Why was her grief so much more poignant than that of others? How was she so much more attached to Jesus than anyone else?

52

There is in existence a remnant of a "Gospel According to Mary" that notes that she understood more deeply what Jesus was actually teaching than the male disciples whose intuitive minds were too limited to grasp the mystical aspects. Sometime after the Resurrection appearance, she is reported to have addressed and comforted them.

THE GOSPEL OF MARY

❖ Ask for volunteers to read this conversation among Jesus, the disciples, and Mary. Have someone be the narrator, Jesus, Peter, and Mary. The rest of the group can be the chorus of disciples, or the narrator can read that brief part while the group observes.

❖ How does this ancient writing influence what you think about the relationship between Mary and Jesus and between Mary and the disciples? What do you think of the idea that Mary was an actual disciple who might have had a leadership role? That Jesus loved her more than he loved

The Gospel of Mary

When the blessed one had said this [do not be discouraged], He greeted them all, saying, "Peace be with you. Receive my peace to yourselves. Beware that no one lead you astray, saying 'Lo here!' or 'Lo there!' for the Son of Man is within you. Follow after Him! Those who seek Him will find Him. Go then and preach the gospel of the kingdom. Do no lay down any rules beyond what I appointed for you, and do not give a law like the lawgiver lest you be constrained by it." When he said this, He departed.

But they were grieved. They wept greatly, saying, "How shall we go to the gentiles and preach the gospel of the kingdom of the Son of Man? If they did not spare him, how will they spare us?" Then Mary stood up, greeted them all, and said to her brethren, "Do not weep and do not grieve nor be irresolute, for His grace will be entirely with you and will protect you. But rather let us praise His greatness, for He has prepared us and made us into men." When Mary said this, she turned their hearts to the Good, and they began to discuss the words of the [Savior].

Peter said to Mary, "Sister, we know that the Saviour loved you more than the rest of women. Tell us the words of the Saviour which you remember—which you know (but) we do not, nor have we heard them."

the other women who followed him?

❖ What do you suppose is meant by Mary's comment that "He has prepared us and made us into men"?

Mary answered and said, "What is hidden from you I will proclaim to you." And she began to speak to them these words: "I," she said, "I saw the Lord in a vision. . . . He answered and said to me, 'Blessed are you that you did not waver at the sight of me. For where the mind is, there is the treasure.' "

(From the Nag Hammadi Library, translated by James M. Robinson.)

Mary was hardly thinking of theology at that lonely moment in the garden. She was not interested in who would assume leadership. She was not thinking of the role of women in Israel's history or of her new status as a bereaved woman. She was groping for any prop to hold her up in the face of this double disaster, and she groped her way toward the cave and met the unexpected.

Messengers of Light

MESSENGERS OF LIGHT
Paint or draw pictures of angels as you might see them. Or do a collage of such pictures from cards or magazines.

Or, check www.peaceangels.org to see the drawings by Lin Evola. Using craft supplies or ordinary "stuff" that you might otherwise discard, make your own peace angel.

Two figures draped in white were seated on the shelf of the tomb. The text describes them as angels, messengers of God to Mary alone (John 20:11-12).

The idea of angels has captured the imagination of people in new ways over the past few years. Angels seem to symbolize the power of God's presence in our lives. One of my new friends is a professional artist whose vision and angelic encounter have led to the Peace Angel Project. Lin Evola's goal is to sculpt larger-than-human-size angels out of melted armaments and to place them in the troubled spots of the earth as a call to peace. The sketches and initial figures that she showed to me were powerful images of heavenly intercession.

This Gospel story may be the only time an angel has made a biblical appearance without the initial greeting, "Fear not." Perhaps the angels realized that Mary's fear was not of them and that they were unlikely to add to it. They did not tell her what she asked of them. They gave her no word of resolution. They had not been there when Peter went in, and there was no way they could have walked around her after he left. All they asked was why she was weeping (John 20:13).

Poor Mary! In her anguish, she spoke her loss: gone, all gone! And she whirled around at the advent of another stranger, only to be asked the same question by another blurred figure (John 20:14-15). How could she fulfill her duty to the dead if the body was missing? Where could he be?

The Encounter

There is something heart wrenching about seeing another's grief, and all the grief and loss that we have stuffed into dark corners of our own life come pouring out in sympathy. Perhaps that was why so many Americans wept over the loss of the British Princess Diana. With all the friends I have lost to AIDS, I cannot be near the AIDS quilt without tears of grief. Imagine the compassion awakened in Jesus to see before him the evidence of Mary's loss of him. And so he spoke her name—just that (John 20:15-16).

❖ Read John 20:11-13. Compare the same story in the other three Gospels: Matthew 28:1-8; Mark 16:1-8; Luke 24:1-7. How does the Gospel writer identify the angels? What difference, if any, would it make to the story or to you if these beings were men (Mark and Luke) rather than angels (Matthew and John)?

THE ENCOUNTER

❖ Have you ever had an encounter with someone you believed to be an angel? If so, what was the occasion and what happened? What consequences did that encounter have?

❖ Read John 20:15-17. Imagine yourself in this setting.

Journal for yourself the dialogue you might like to have with Jesus in the garden. Who would he see if he looked into your soul? What would you ask him to bless or change, to clear or heal? Can his compassion accept you as you are? Can yours?

❖ Think of yourself as a witness at a trial or accident of some kind. What sorts of things are important to recall?

❖ Now think about having been a witness as Mary was, charged with delivering the news to the other disciples. What sense of importance might you feel? What sense of urgency might you experience? Might you have some understanding of being on the brink of something

And he looked at her, really saw her. One of Jesus' greatest gifts to those close to him was his ability to see past the masks of social propriety and to see into the soul as he did when he first met Peter (John 1:42). The English says, "He brought Simon to Jesus, who looked at him." The Greek says he "looked into him."

As Mary wiped the tears from her eyes, she saw him too; and she recognized him when he spoke her name. She cried out in her native Aramaic. The shock must have been huge, the blast of joy incandescent. The first thing Mary did was to reach out for him—something no woman of her time would have done to a man unless it had been a gesture previously allowed.

And here the line was drawn for her. With all the emotional roller coaster of the past three days, this was the marker of a new relationship with a new person in a new reality. The paradigm had shifted. Jesus could no longer be touched. He told Mary the message that needed to be passed on to the disciples. He called them his brothers. He made it clear that his time upon the earth was limited, and he was preparing to leave. But he wanted to be very clear that where he was going was to a shared reality, "to my Father and your Father, to my God and your God" (John 20:17).

Nothing more was reported of what was spoken between them, nothing of how Mary dried her face on her skirt or tried to explain what she was doing there. No more about the angels left sitting in

much larger and more influential than just reporting a single event? How does this change your understanding of Mary's encounter? What difference, if any, does it make in how you understand your own responsibility to witness to what you know of the risen Christ?

THE LIVING CHRIST

❖ Talk about changes in relationships you have had. What were the "markers" in your awareness?

❖ Tell your own stories. How does the sharing of your own learning help others learn? What have you learned from hearing others' stories?

Using your hymnal, search for Holy Week and Easter hymns that deal with the relationship of Jesus with his disciples and with us. Sing or say several of these hymns. How

the tomb, no comment about Mary's anxious glance at Jesus' wounds to reassure herself of his healing. Nothing of her hungry gaze at the face that only moments earlier she had thought lost forever. We are told only that she went.

At the time, hurrying along the same route on which she stumbled a short time earlier, carrying the same package of spices, Mary could have had no inkling of the importance of what she had been told to do and say. For in those moments of excitement and purpose, Mary's steps and words carried her onto the world stage as the first witness of the Resurrection with the first commission to bear that word to others (John 20:17-18).

The Living Christ

If seeing Jesus alive again transformed Mary from grief-stricken woman to evangelist, might seeing God face to face also transform us? The ancients said such an experience would kill someone. Our inner person, the ego, perceives it as a death, as annihilation worse than death. If we walk into whatever is our equivalent of a burning bush (Exodus 3:2) or "a refiner's fire" (Malachi 3:2), our ego thinks we are committing a violent act against it. In a way, that is true; for the old self cannot survive in the refiner's fire. If that encounter seems to us to be a death-and-resurrection, what higher self might emerge from the ashes of the old controlling ego?

57

do they convey the emotive impact of Jesus' separation from the disciples and they from him? Is there any sense in which their experience is your own? If so, how, and what impact does it have on your faith?

What science fiction stories have helped you to think creatively about miracles and possibilities? In the world of fiction, we can try out ideas and concepts without threat. Stories that seemed fantastic a hundred years ago detail inventions that we take for granted now. Think about some of Jules Verne's amazing forward thinking and how the objects he envisioned came into being. Read more of Frank Herbert's work and think about how those tales influence your understanding of faith.

❖ Have someone take notes on a flipchart as the group shares words or phrases indicating the ways in which religious objects have been turned into idols. As you look at the list, talk about what the right

Jesus himself was left standing in that garden with a new future to comprehend. David La Chapelle in his parable of a man's spiritual journey entitled *A Voice on the Wind* (Gateway Productions, 1995) teaches that "only those who can feel the hope of the future have the courage to undo the knots of the past. If you are to sing free of fear, sing free of suffering, then you must catch the dreams of your people and dissolve them, liberating their future" (page 123).

Jesus' words to Mary and the message to the disciples indicated his understanding of his new state. People have wondered how much Jesus actually understood of the process that moved him from man to *Christos*. In his classic science fiction novels about *Dune* (Ace Books), author Frank Herbert wove a tale of the evolution of awareness and awakening in the young man, Paul Atreides, who becomes that story's messiah. Herbert traces throughout the novels the whole picture of having certain legends firmly in place, of the awakening "interiority" of the man's awareness beyond normal. Other people see this as a form of magic. He sees it as a call to "terrible purpose." Paul outlines the gift of observation that sees both miniscule changes and global possibilities. He lists the growing understanding of a cosmology and a growing compulsion to teach others. And he recognizes the need for events that trigger both the inner awareness and the outer perception. It is a fascinating study of what might possibly have been part of Jesus' life.

relationship to those items might be.

What happens when people's respect for a religious practice or item becomes idolatry? As you grow in your relationship with the living Christ, what kind of balance and under-standing might you need? How might you become a help and a light to those caught in the possession of idolatry?

❖ As you end this session, spend a moment in silent prayer together affirm-ing your place in your own faith tradition and committing yourself once again to the highest and best good to which God has called you. As you pray, take time, if you feel called, to make or affirm your commit-ment to Jesus Christ.

Perhaps Jesus knew in those moments alone in the garden that there was no way really to share what he had experienced. He may have wanted to let people know that death could no longer hurt them. He may have wanted to break the old superstitions that allowed people to be controlled by old religions and old gods. And he may have realized finally that there was no way to convince the disciples that they too could pass through the "valley of the shadow" and be revived. We can only wonder whether he foresaw their lack of comprehension, their all-too-human need for a hero on a pedestal rather than a model to be fol-lowed. For here, in the garden, the man of Galilee was made Lord and Christ by his resurrection.

CHAPTER FIVE

The Power of Spiritual Community
Acts 2:1-43

PURPOSE
The purpose of this session is to see the Pentecost experience as a modern possibility, to find new ways to move forward with the Holy Spirit.

THE SESSION PLAN
Choose from among the core teaching activities (identified with ❖) and add options in **bold italics** to extend beyond a 45-60 minute session.

AFTER THE RISING
❖ Read Acts 2:1-43. What part of this story strikes you with new emphasis in this reading? How does that new experience mark for you ways in which you have changed since you last read it with attention?

After the Rising

Fifty days have gone by since the tomb was found empty, fifty wildly exciting, totally confusing, then long-drawn-out days of uncertainty. The stories in the various Gospels tell us of the encounter in the upper room on the first evening (John 20:19-23), of the walk down the road to Emmaus (Luke 24:13-35), of the meeting in the upper room a week later when Jesus allowed Thomas to touch him (John 20:24-29).

The disciples needed to know that the risen Christ was not a ghost. You cannot touch ghosts. It was too disconcerting to have this person disappearing after breaking bread, showing up through closed doors, then turning up on the shore at Galilee for breakfast (John 21:1-14). There were chances to talk with Jesus then, but the answers to their questions were more confusing than ever. The only hope they held on to was that Jesus told them there would be the coming of the Holy Spirit. (See John 14:25-26.) What did that mean?

❖ Now read each of the Scripture passages mentioned in the first paragraph of the section "After the Rising" individually or shared among small groups. Afterward, read all of Acts 2 together. How might you connect with the experience of the author? What questions are raised for you?

Numbers of people have had experiences of some kind of visitation after someone they loved has died. Share those stories with one another, listening to them with the same courtesy and focus that you used in your exercise of Appreciative Inquiry.

Or, if you prefer, have a campfire and tell ghost stories.

A DIFFERENT KINGDOM
Discuss your image of "kingdom." What is the classical theological idea about that word? Having lived in a federal republic based on the concept of democracy all your life, how does that word strike you now? (If you have lived in a monarchy or other form of

With the advantage of 20-20 hindsight, we may think we can pull the stories together into some meaningful whole. But there are still gaps and questions and reality shifts that make no sense, then or now. Logic stumbles. And faith is a very subjective viewpoint.

What was it Jesus expected them to do when he was gone? There had been that odd conversation when the mother of James and John asked for privilege of power and place in the Kingdom that Jesus kept trying to explain. Basically, he told them they were way off base (Matthew 20:20-23). They did not understand. The only kind of kingdom they had ever seen was all about being important, about having power and running the country. All the instructions reported by Matthew seemed contradictory in the face of the reality in which they lived. "Cure the sick, raise the dead, cleanse the lepers, cast out demons" (Matthew 10:8). Raise the dead? Who, me?

A Different Kind of Kingdom

I have witnessed during these past few years the creation of a "chaordic organization"—one that blends order and chaos to form an organizational system that works. I have shared in the amount of time and energy it has taken to build the United Religions Initiative. I can sympathize with the disciples. They did not have a Chaordic Alliance to help them understand the internal processes of a corporate structure with no power

61

government, how does that influence your concept of "kingdom"?)

❖ What kind of power does "kingdom" represent as a form of government or as a theocracy (a nation ruled by God)? What do you think Jesus meant by his kingdom? What did it mean to the people of his time? How have you experienced "the kingdom of God" in your own life?

❖ A "chaordic organization" is one based on the tension between chaos and order. In other words, it begins as a free-for-all discussion; and out of that chaos it begins to reveal its own working order. It works on the same theory as the math that produced the fractal patterns you may have seen during your study of Chapter One. What might your job look like if your company or organization allowed itself to redesign according to the input from all the workers?

pyramid. They had never heard of dreaming international relationships from the function of Appreciative Inquiry. They were having enough trouble understanding a single man who could be flesh and blood one day, dead the next, resurrected the day after, and disappeared into clouds a few weeks later—gone again, with no hope of his turning up suddenly to help sort out things. And so they were sitting in the upper room fifty days after the Resurrection when the impossible happened.

The morning sun assaults my eyes
As I step from the dim shadows of an
upper room,
A place of hiding, shrinking, waiting,
Driven out by the compulsion
Born of an eerie flame.
We sat together, as always,
Wondering. What would become of us.
Tore bread, waited, tore mind.
In the swirl of her skirt
As she passed me by
A light was ignited above
The head of my sane, normal friend.
Therefore, not he, but I in question.
Running amid the sudden voices
To the morning sun.

My eyes water with the shock of light,
Perhaps with the shock within.
Can it be that I see the gathering
Of a crowd, strangers all,
Threatening? Curious?
From all points of the compass.
Chattering in the tongues of half the
world,
Listening.
Suddenly the disparate pieces

Of talk, memory, schoolboy recitation,
Fall together in my mind.
The picture from the puzzle:
The face of my lost Lord, grieved,
Gone, surrounded by letters of flame,
Familiar words.
And by the locking of the missing piece
A flare of understanding.
His spirit commands my body.
An arm raises.
A mouth speaks.
I, Peter

[AVR 2-26-87]

This poem was a gift of inspiration when the story was much on my mind. **Write your own poem about the Pentecost experience.**

The Wind and Fire of God

WIND AND FIRE

❖ Biblical characters seem to like to go into the wind and clouds. Form three groups, if you have enough people, and assign Matthew 17:1-13 to one group; 2 Kings 2:1-12 to the next; Acts 1:1-11 to the third. Use drama or other artistic method to recreate your scene.

❖ What do these stories reveal to you about the power of God? Had you been a disciple at the time, what questions would these amazing events have raised for you? How do they influence your faith now?

Forty days of appearances following the Crucifixion with more teaching, the presentation of "convincing proofs," and then a dramatic departure into the clouds (Acts 1:1-9). Was Jesus gone for good now? No, it could not be.

In the same mind-boggling epiphany that Peter, James, and John had had at the Transfiguration (Matthew 17:1-13), two dazzling "men" stood this time before all the remaining disciples to declare, "Men of Galilee, why do you stand looking up toward heaven? This Jesus, who has been taken up from you into heaven, will come in the same way as you saw him go into heaven" (Acts 1:10-11).

First Elijah (2 Kings 2:1-12), then Elijah with Moses (Matthew 17:3-8), now Jesus disappearing into the clouds! What next? Ten days later, they would find out. Gathered for the festival of Pentecost, the disciples were overcome by the rush of wind and the flame of God's Spirit fire.

Have the local rabbi share with your class about the feast of Shavuot. What did that festival look like in Jerusalem? What was the crowd doing? Ask him or her to talk about relevant passages from his or her Scripture.

Moved to speak so all could hear—Galilean and foreigner alike—these men were witnesses to the powerful presence of God (Acts 2:1-12).

Amazing! Astonishing! Perplexing! How can this be? As always, one contingent sneered with the assumption of a simple explanation: These guys are drunk.

Drunk before breakfast? Oh, no. It was that wind, those puzzle pieces that made sudden sense. It was all that Jesus had tried to explain—illuminated by the inward flame, the recognition. John told us that Jesus' breath had been given to the disciples after the Resurrection. The Spirit of God was already with them. This was the igniting of purpose as the disciples were utterly transformed by a singular awareness of the power and abiding presence of God.

A GOOD SERMON
❖ Read Acts 2:14-36. Note also the passages from Joel 2 and from Psalm 16 to see how they are included and changed.

❖ How would you summarize Peter's sermon? How does it speak to current issues and to future ones? How is it prophetic? Gracious? Challenging? Provoking? If you had

A Mighty Good Sermon

This was the "ah-ha" of what it had all been about and what they were to do next. In that moment of clarity, Peter's speech (Acts 2:14-36) was heard by a crowd of people gathered in Jerusalem for Shavuot. With wonder, they heard and understood: These were familiar words of Scripture. Peter gave them a portion of Psalm 16 and claimed it as a foretelling of the Resurrection. He translated their experience of the coming of the Spirit into the prophecy from Joel (2:28-32). He enumerated the ways in which the life, death, and resurrection of Jesus ful-

been part of the power structure, what might your response have been? How does this Pentecost experience "fire you up" to do God's work?

filled the scriptural descriptions of messiah. With growing confidence Peter spoke his witness to "know with certainty that God has made him both Lord and Messiah, this Jesus whom you crucified" (Acts 2:36).

In Whose Language?

While I was in seminary, one of my professors was fascinated by *glossolalia,* the pattern of utterance known as "speaking in tongues." (Paul describes it as a spiritual gift in 1 Corinthians 14, adding that it has value when someone is available to interpret.) The professor played a tape for us that had been recorded during a service in a Pentecostal congregation, and I listened with a musician's ear to the rise and fall of sounds that seemed to have no linguistic meaning. It was quite different from the descriptions of the abilities attributed to parapsychological channeling that allow someone to speak a foreign language he or she had not learned.

Weeks later when I visited in a nursing home, I was introduced to a woman whose cognitive language skills had deteriorated with senility. With a smile and a graceful handshake, she spoke pleasantly in meaningless syllables that rose and fell in the same pattern as the voices on the professor's tape.

What happened on that Day of Pentecost was described very differently; Peter was speaking in his own known language. Those present heard through

What impact did this exercise have on your appreciation of the power of language to convey the faith?

(Next Pentecost in your church try doing this exercise by having people stand around the perimeter of the congregation so that the people present can hear the various languages as each voice enters. Readers may bring family Bibles from their countries of origin or copies of foreign language Bibles from the local library.)

HOLY ADVOCATE
❖ Choose your favorite disciple of Jesus and talk about your choice. What appealed to you and why?

❖ Think about someone who has modeled faith, constancy, and leadership for you. (This person does not have to be a church member.) What is it about this role model that has inspired you? How has he or she discerned God's claim and then acted upon it? What obstacles has

those sounds texts that had meaning for them—"their own tongue"—and they understood at a deeper level the message of hope and prophecy. The festival called Pentecost would never be the same again.

Holy Advocate

The jewel of the teaching had now been given its setting, its framework. Not only was the dead rabbi risen, it had all been foretold, prophesied. Its divine significance was thereby proved. The Holy Spirit, which Jesus called the Advocate, had granted Peter the power to advocate indeed.

Dear Peter, *Petros,* the rock—one of Jesus' favorite puns. Throughout the Gospels, Peter was the realist, slow to grasp the intuitive. There were times when, using Christian author Frederick Buechner's words in *Peculiar Treasures* (Harper & Row, 1979, page 135), "Peter said the wrong thing . . . or asked the wrong question, or got the wrong point, or at least failed to do the thing that was right. The day he saw Jesus walking on the water and tried to walk out to him himself, for instance, he was just about to go under for the third time because rocks have never been much good at floating when Jesus came to the rescue (Matthew 14:28-31)."

Despite the nickname Jesus gave Simon bar Jonah, Peter seemed not to perceive himself in the role of spokesperson or leader. He just did what he felt his

this person overcome? What have you learned from your observance of and relationship with him or her?

Use a Bible diction-ary to learn more about the roles of priests and Levites. Then stage a debate about the roles of priests and prophets and the requirements for the jobs. Why would the Jews have made those jobs hereditary? Should the church depend on "preacher's kids" to carry on the work? Or should ministry be affirmed as a calling of the Holy Spirit to indi-viduals? How has your faith tradition affirmed calls to ministry?

Journaling exercise: How has the Holy Spirit empowered your ministry in the world?

Lord had called him to do. Peter could not have imagined the day when "the shoes of the Fisherman" would be one of the titles used to describe the heritage and power of the pope of a Roman Catholic Church that covered the globe. Aside from the hereditary roles of priest and Levite or the schools of the prophets, this was the first mass experience of humans being empowered to do God's work.

The Spirit came not just to the chosen, the educated, or even just the men. The gift was offered to the sons and daugh-ters, the gift that Jesus called the Advocate. In the name lay the message. Bishop Shamana reminds us, "When we make these connections to direct know-ing in the setting of the church and faith community, what joy we feel in the cor-porate consciousness that shares spiritual unity and power. We feel the presence of the early church and the Spirit power Jesus promised at his ascension" (*Seeing in the Dark;* Abingdon, 2001, pages 64–65).

A legend. A setting. A prophecy ful-filled. A purpose. In the aftermath of the event itself, the disciples of Jesus began to recall things Jesus had said and to construct some kind of future for them-selves. Tell the story, and what a story it is! Pass on the teaching. Well, how does that happen? Who has the right to tell the story? And which version was true and which was not? And so it began.

Throughout twenty centuries people for whom the story was true, people empowered by the Holy Spirit in their

❖ Look back over the major events of Christian history or of world history in which Christianity played a significant role. What does this retrospective view reveal? Who has advocated for what in the name of God and what have been some of the consequences? Who has lived or died because of doing so? What legacy has the church today inherited? How does that affect us as the church today? How does that affect you?

own time, took up the role of advocate. They tried in each century to cleanse the later accretions and go back to that day in Jerusalem. They tried in a million ways to live out the teachings of Jesus, to discern what he said and what someone else said he said. They tried to sit on hillsides and wait for his return. They tried over and over to use Jesus' name to justify actions and words that had no basis in his reality. They claimed to have the truth, and they demonstrated in a hundred ways that there was no truth in them. They murdered and destroyed and crusaded in the name of God.

As we sit with the weight of two thousand years of Christian history on our shoulders and look at the original story, can we see the disparity? Where in this first sermon of the movement not yet called Christianity did the word *faith* occur? Where was the limit set on who was allowed to experience the Holy Spirit? Who held the keys to the Kingdom to lock in or lock out? And where is that exclusivistic four-letter word *only?*

A NEW FLAME
Together research various spiritual practices and share the findings. Which ones are new to you? Which ones have worked for you? As you grow in your understanding of yourself and your own spiritual needs, which practices appeal to you to draw you onward?

A New Flame

In this beginning of the twenty-first century, counting slightly off from the year of Jesus' birth, we are living into the shift of paradigm. As we relive and relearn the Scriptures in the light of the Advocate, we can experience again the empowerment of Spirit. Rabbi Lerner, author of *Spirit Matters* (Hampton Roads, 2000), reminds us, "Building a spiritually

❖ Do an Appreciative Inquiry exercise. Have someone record on a chalkboard or large piece of paper the ideas that come out of this discussion. This is an exercise in dreaming.

What would your community look like if it lived by the highest and best gifts of everyone? If every child in your community were raised with love and positive self-esteem, allowed to develop his or her creative gifts, what might your future look like? If you were to build a spiritual community across the lines of color or faith tradition, what values could you share in common? If the "creative child" within each one of you could dream the best possible world, what might that look like?

Ask a volunteer to type up, photocopy, and distribute copies of the idea list to everyone. Put that list on your bathroom mirror or refrigerator door and read it as if the things

centered community means incorporating spiritual practices at each stage and staying focused on the highest goals for which the community is being built" (page 290).

I have been a witness to such a scene as Peter experienced. I have been one in a crowd of people from all corners of the earth upon whom the fire of Spirit and purpose and advocacy has fallen. Let me paint the picture.

With the preparation for the celebration of the fiftieth anniversary of the United Nations in San Francisco, Bishop William Swing, episcopal leader of the diocese, awoke to his new vision. If in fifty years the nations had not made a workable peace, it had much to do with the problem of religion. A small gathering in June 1996 led to a larger conference in June 1997. Two hundred guests from all points of the compass, of all ages, of all faith traditions, came together at Stanford for a week. The question: Was it possible to create an organization that would provide a safe space for permanent, daily dialogue among the religions of the world? Were we crazy? Could it be done?

Through the process of Appreciative Inquiry, the days grew toward a unanimous "Yes." On the final evening at a banquet for all, the last sharing was done by one of the African delegates who asked us to celebrate with him in dance. Everybody up! As we moved to the rhythm of his drum, he turned and pushed the button of a boom box; and there were 250 people in saris, dashikis,

on the list had already happened. Then notice when things start to happen!

Use various art or craft materials, music, dance, or some other creative medium to illustrate one item on the list.

To see the Charter of United Religions Initiative, with all of its preamble, purpose, and principles, visit the website at www.uri.org.

A NEW WORLD
❖ Review Acts 2:1-21 and Joel 2:28-32, paying particular attention to the world these prophets envisioned. What would it take, do you think, for this

monks robes, business suits, silk dresses, nuns habits, and blue jeans doing the Macarena—and giggling! The energy in that garden lit up the sky.

As my observant mind woke to what I was witnessing, I recognized that I had seen the end of the world. I felt like Simeon who felt he could die in peace for having held the infant Savior (Luke 2:25-33). Nothing could ever be the same in a world where shared laughter could break down the centuries-old walls of suspicion and hatred. The old order was ended. We had danced it into dust.

The future, in the rhythm of the Advocate, is being built upon that shared laughter and vision. The work that followed, the crafting of a chaordic organization in which all voices and traditions are honored, led to the signing of the Charter of the United Religions Initiative in June 2000.

The Preamble of the Charter begins, "We, people of diverse religions, spiritual expressions and indigenous traditions throughout the world, hereby establish the United Religions Initiative to promote enduring, daily interfaith cooperation, to end religiously motivated violence, and to create cultures of peace, justice and healing for the Earth and all living beings."

A New World

Peter, who stood on the steps in the midst of Jerusalem during the Feast of Weeks (Pentecost), newly empowered

vision to come to fruition? What part can you play, individually and as part of the church, to bring about this vision?

❖ Tell "ah ha" stories. How has the Holy Spirit guided, surprised, inspired, or enabled you to help bring about God's kingdom?

Use your hymnal to locate hymns and prayers about the Holy Spirit. Sing or say together several of them, such as "Holy Spirit, Come, Confirm Us" or "Spirit of Faith, Come Down." How does the musical setting convey the faith truth? What are the verbs in the lyrics and how do they reveal the way God works through us? Take some time in song or prayer to open and commit yourself to the Spirit's leading.

with vision and purpose, newly convicted with the vision of his friend and teacher as the Anointed One, could not see down the ages. He would have shuddered if he knew of the hatred and judgmentalism, the cruelty and inhumane treatment, people would impose on one another in the name of the Christ. He might have agreed that Christ was only for those Jews who were there, only for those who agreed with the accolade of Messiah for the teacher Jesus. But Peter himself was given a further dream that opened the future to people of other nations and faiths (Acts 10).

Peter's experience of "ah-ha" was not a wall to shut out people. It was an experience of illumination, of transcendence, of implosion. "You are the light of the world. . . . Let your light shine before others, so that they may see your good works and give glory to your Father in heaven" (Matthew 5:14-16). Glory is light; light to light to light. Enlighten the world.

We are called by our belief in the "ah-ha" that Peter shared that day, that Jesus is Lord, to bring our light to the world. In his name we are called to be a spiritual community. As we build a new world on a new paradigm of cooperation instead of competition, of values instead of price, we are building a world in which *Spirit Matters.*

In his book of that title, Rabbi Michael Lerner outlines ways in which we can reconstruct the institutions by which our world is ordered.

If we learn from the lessons of

**Read and discuss the
book Spirit Matters.**
In what ways do
Lerner's suggestions
match the ideals of
Christian teaching?
How might you use his
ideas to improve your
area of work?

Closing Meditation:
❖ Invoke the presence
of God among you.
Take turns sharing an
experience of new
understanding that has
come from this study.
What new options and
ideas have come your
way? How might you
change your spiritual
disciplines?

Spend a few minutes
lifting up the needs
and joys of those
about whom you care.
Send blessings to
those whose names
are raised—and send
your blessings to all of
creation.

Accept again the com-
mitment to listen for
the Holy Spirit in your
life as you make deci-
sions and choices.
Share a group hug—
and laugh together.

**Throw a party for the
whole church school
to celebrate the time
you have spent
together.**

Creation about the genius of those first single-celled creatures, we will experience life through a "permeable membrane." The membrane allowed them to take in everything that passed by, keep what was nourishing, and excrete what was toxic. Why would we allow anyone else to feed us the poisons of judgment, prejudice, hatred, isolationism, and negativity? Why would we accept negative judgments of ourselves when we have the innate wisdom to recognize their toxicity? The permeable membrane of the first single-celled creatures that allowed them to discern nourishment and toxicity also allowed them to cooperate and specialize so that creatures like you and me could exist. Our bodies are miracles worthy of radical amazement.

How might our lives shift if we took seriously the gift of the Holy Spirit to advocate for the world? What gifts have we hidden under the bushel of our fears? What goodness has been lost as we hide our true selves to escape the judgment of other human beings? As disciples of Christ called to grow in spirit and in truth, how shall we live out the dream of a kingdom based on love and cooperation?

In this new millennium, we have a chance to start anew, to keep what is nourishing and to discard what has been toxic. We have a chance to find the other cooperative cells of love and shared values and join together to evolve a new world that is based on the best we have to give rather than the worst. We are called to be true to the wisdom of God.